ACT BEFORE YOU *over*THINK

*Make Decisions Easier And
Liberate Your Mind*

Lison Mage

Published by The Mindful Experience Pty Ltd, Manly, Australia
Contact contact@lisonmage.com

Copyright © 2022 Lison Mage

All rights reserved. Except as permitted under the Australian Copyright Act 1968, no part of this publication may be reproduced, stored in a retrieval system, or transmitted in any form or by any means, electronic, mechanical, photocopying, recording or otherwise, without prior written permission from the publisher. All enquiries should be made to the author.

The moral rights of the authors have been asserted.

Author: Lison Mage
Co-author: Guy Langlois
Title: *Act Before You overThink: Make Decisions Easier And Liberate Your Mind*
ISBN: 978-0-6452330-0-1
Subjects: Self-Help Techniques | Psychology | Decision-Making
Book Editor: Jeanie Keogh
Illustrator: Pierre Langlois
Cover Designer: Mary Ann Smith
Book Proofreader: Anita Saunders

 A catalogue record for this work is available from the National Library of Australia

Disclaimer:
The material in this publication is of the nature of general comment only and does not represent professional advice. All material for educational purposes only. We recommend to always seek the advice of a qualified professional before making any decision regarding personal and business needs. To the maximum extent permitted by law, the authors and publisher disclaim all responsibility and liability to any person arising directly or indirectly from any person taking or not taking action based on the information in this publication.

Thank You

To my co-author Guy Langlois. Without his organisation, research skills and support, this book would simply not exist.

To my family, that kept encouraging us during this adventure.

To our dedicated editor Jeanie Keogh, who challenged us with questions and remarks, spreading words of encouragement along the way.

To our talented illustrator Pierre Langlois, who put all his heart into crafting beautiful drawings and helped us put my concepts into compelling visuals.

To our patient cover designer Mary Ann Smith, who designed a fantastic cover, encapsulating our book's essence.

To our detail-oriented proofreader Anita Saunders, who helped us put the final touches to the manuscript.

To you, the reader, for picking this book and sharing this journey with me.

Acknowledgement

In order to write this book, I conducted extensive research, interviewing more than 365 participants who generously took the time to answer my questions and share their overthinking journey.

A specific section at the end of the book mentions these contributors (when they allow me to do so) who shared their valuable insights.

Please note that throughout this book, I will present stories of overthinkers. These are in no way direct transcriptions of confidential exchanges with interviewees. The characters and events depicted in these "overthinker stories" are entirely fictitious. They are built from my research, combined with several interviews' findings, where details and situations are altered and mixed up to ensure anonymity. Their sole purpose is to illustrate a concept linked to overthinking.

Testimonials

"When Lison mentioned this topic I was immediately curious. As engineers we pride ourselves in thinking deeply about problems but are we in fact overthinking?
And the answer is—sometimes! I really recommend Lison's book for its practical techniques backed by insightful analysis and all in an easy-to-access format."
—**Dr Bronwyn Evans**, FIEAust FTSE, CEO of Engineers Australia.

"Mage provides an impressive evidence base and uses analogies and creative narratives to unlock the issues of overthinking. She lands the solution with a compelling and pragmatic approach to making decisions efficiently, even the hardest ones! A must-read for corporate leaders and influencers."
—**Bryan Whitefield**, Speaker, facilitator and author of *Risky Business and Persuasive Advising*.

"The idea of managing our own mind in order to activate the best version of ourselves is something we need to focus on in our complicated world. Lison has given us a very practical and clarifying way of thinking about the habit of overthinking. There are clear "myths of overthinking" as Lison powerfully calls out, that can lead us to get caught in using overthinking as a strategy. If this is you, this book will

help you find out the ways in which you can regain control of your habits."
—**Dr Amy Silver**, Expert in high-performance work cultures, and author of best-selling book, *The Loudest Guest: How to change and control your relationship with fear.*

"When deep and creative thinking is core to what you do daily, it is easy for your ideas to spiral and lose what is important. With so many of us caught up in our heads, there has never been a better time for this insightful book on overthinking. But be careful, don't overthink it! Instead, enjoy the evidence-based insights that Lison presents into this fascinating phenomenon."
—**Dr Jenine Beekhuyzen**, Founder of the Tech Girls Movement Foundation and CEO of Adroit Research.

"We meet over 1,000 entrepreneurs a year globally and we can confirm that overthinking by entrepreneurs directly correlates to venture failure rates. We would recommend this book to all of our venture founders."
—**Founders at Catallyze.**

Table of Contents

Introduction	1
First Myth: Overthinking is Enhancing my Thinking	7
Chapter 1 - Finding the Tipping Point of Excellence	12
Chapter 2 - Removing the Resolution Blindfold	28
Chapter 3 - Mastering Mental Time Travel	45
Conclusion of the First Myth	62
Second Myth: Overthinking is Inconsequential to Me	65
Chapter 4 - Addressing the Elephant in the Room	68
Chapter 5 - Dispelling the Lies of the Self	86
Chapter 6 - Navigating the Paths to Progress	104
Conclusion of the Second Myth	119
Third Myth: Overthinking is Inevitable in Decision-Making	122
Chapter 7 - Trusting the Process	127
Chapter 8 - Trading up Decisions Reversibility	144
Chapter 9 - Thriving With Core Values	164
Conclusion of the Third Myth	180

Conclusion	184
Working With Me	188
Interview Contributors	191
Bibliography	197

Introduction

If you were constantly living with some background noise, like indistinct chatter or traffic noise, would you notice it?

I lived in the peaceful South of France until my early 20s, then I moved to Shanghai, spending three years in the Middle Country. There, I was immersed in a city that never sleeps. Almost everything you could think of is accessible every day of the week, 24 hours a day.

At the time, the local news reported that more than 10 million people commuted daily in the city's metro and its 400 stations. An unfathomable number of cars and scooters were constantly honking to signal their presence to others. The wind whipped through the endless streets and echoed the whole city's agitation and ruckus.

And yet, after a few months, I didn't notice the "background noise" anymore.

I only realised when I went for an excursion in the Chinese countryside to explore the breathtaking Luxi Gorge. Walking along a peaceful river by day, we stopped at a small cabin in the middle of nowhere, and I slept on bamboo sticks, which was a memorable experience, especially for my back!

Surrounded by silence, my ears were ringing. It was as if I could not tolerate the surreal calm of the place. Eventually, something popped, and the noise disappeared, allowing me to experience pure bliss.

Scientists studied this phenomenon, called auditory habituation, or in other words, how we adapt to ambient noise.

In their experiments, they exposed mice to a constant, loud but harmless noise (similar to a lawnmower or hairdryer) for a week. Then, they compared their brain activity with those of mice that remained in a quiet environment. The scientists noticed a reduction in the number of neurotransmitters released in the auditory cortex, which meant that the sounds heard were not transmitted entirely[1].

Researchers tested how fast humans can adapt to ambient noise in an open office space and found it happens pretty quickly: in less than 20 minutes[2], in fact. But unfortunately, even if we can filter out unwanted sounds, they can still have a negative impact on us.

According to the World Health Organisation, prolonged or excessive exposure to noise, whether in the community or at work, can cause permanent medical conditions, such as hypertension and ischemic heart disease[3].

When Spanish researchers studied the health impact of traffic noise in Madrid, they found associations with increased stress levels, higher risk of depression and cardiovascular issues[4].

So, it appears we can get used to background noise and somehow tolerate it, even if this is detrimental to our wellbeing. And there is another background noise we accept and learn to put up with. It is a mental one and, if you bought this book, you probably know which one I am talking about.

Overthinking is like a persistent noise in your head.

We get so used to it that we don't notice it anymore, even if it drains our strength. When we silence this ceaseless racket, we gain clarity. We feel re-energised yet appeased.

Introduction

But beyond this metaphorical explanation, what is the scientific definition of overthinking? Is it really that bad? It seems there are benefits to overthinking. For instance, to make smarter decisions or ensure we have considered all our options.

With this in mind, I decided to research the difference between thinking and overthinking to see how I could help overthinkers.

I did more than 365 one-on-one interviews with overthinkers over a year. Indeed, this book would not be possible without the many volunteers who generously gave their time. In the end, there were more than 250 hours of qualitative data that I used to investigate this subject and come up with valuable and practical insights.

Based on this interview material, I came to the conclusion that there are three commonly held beliefs about overthinking which are false. I call them the three myths of overthinking. These are:

- Myth 1: Overthinking is enhancing my thinking.
- Myth 2: Overthinking is inconsequential to me.
- Myth 3: Overthinking is inevitable in decision-making.

While conducting my research, I established a scale ranging from 0 to 10, where 0 means not overthinking at all and 10 means overthinking all the time. This enabled both the interviewees and me to rank their level of overthinking.

When asked how they would rank themselves, the participants who believed all three myths ranked their overthinking level at seven or higher.

Those who held fewer beliefs ranked their overthinking level lower. It was particularly striking for the interviewees who viewed themselves as "recovered" overthinkers, namely as those who had successfully conquered their overthinking.

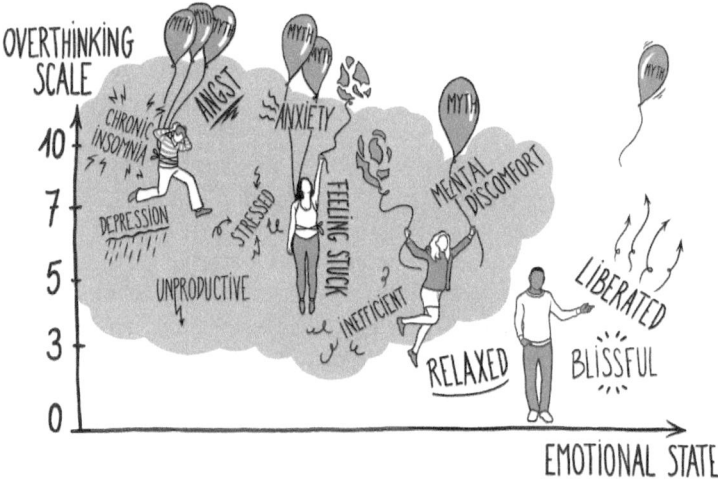

And the higher the level of overthinking, the more the participants were experiencing adverse effects, such as feeling unproductive, inefficient in their decision-making or socially anxious.

At the highest level of overthinking, it's not background noise anymore. Instead, it's a constant aeroplane motor noise that runs in your mind—and it doesn't go unnoticed. People reported experiencing chronic insomnia, crippling levels of stress and anxiety, and mental and physical exhaustion.

So, this book aims to give you the keys to turn down the noise volume, liberate yourself from the shackles of overthinking, and appease your hyperactive mind.

But you might say: "*I don't want to think less; that would make me stupid.*"

You won't.

Conquering overthinking is not about thinking less but thinking better.

Introduction

As you finish this book, your thinking will be sharper and clearer, ensuring you make efficient decisions confidently.

To get these results, we will debunk each of the myths of overthinking, explaining how they form, why they are harmful and the techniques and tools you can use to manage and negate their effects. We will also explore the six different overthinker personas (the Maximiser, the Finisher, the Observer, the Helper, the Dreamer and the Performer) that will help you better identify what triggers your overthinking and the specific behaviours that relate to it.

Finally, as we methodically dismantle these beliefs one by one throughout this book, you will notice yourself overthinking less and less.

Before we begin, here are a few tips to keep in mind to get the most value out of this book.

Firstly, this book is going to challenge you.

I wrote it to be engaging, daring and actionable. However, if you hold any of the false beliefs mentioned above, this will be confronting. The claims made in this book are backed by factual and scientific evidence, as well as my opinions and convictions after spending a great deal of time on this subject. Where research went against my conclusions, I did not exclude it in favour of research that supported my findings.

Secondly, I encourage you to approach the material in this book with a balance of "openness" and "scepticism".

If you find yourself disagreeing with any of the ideas and concepts put forward in this book, try to be open-minded and give them the benefit of the doubt. It could simply be unconscious resistance stemming from your overthinking beliefs.

On the other hand, don't patently agree with everything in this book. There will be sections that resonate with you and others that simply won't. Test and see for yourself what is working best for you.

First Myth

Overthinking is Enhancing my Thinking

As the author Christopher Hitchens aptly said: "*The essence of the independent mind lies not in what it thinks, but in how it thinks.*"

An indispensable prerequisite to any discussion on overthinking is to agree on a standard definition.

Interestingly, there are discrepancies between the generic definition in English dictionaries and psychology literature. The former explains overthinking as "thinking too much about something". The latter calls it "rumination" (relegating "overthinking" to a non-scientific name[1]) and gives at least fourteen different models and theories in an attempt to characterise it[2].

Rather than arbitrarily picking one, I decided to define it with the help of my interviewees, by directly questioning them, asking how they would describe overthinking to a friend who doesn't know what it is.

I was expecting that with such a large number of interviews, I would extract common vocabulary and uncover patterns to synthesise a "generic" definition that most would agree on.

It turned out to be much more complex, somewhat explaining the divergence in the scientific world and the plethora of psychological models.

When asked to define overthinking, most of the answers I got were emotions, symptoms, and situational anecdotes.

Sergey ruminates the same thoughts for hours, which makes him stressed. Paresh cannot sleep as he cannot stop thinking about an upcoming customer meeting. Wendy remembers something awkward she said, and she keeps going over what she should have said instead.

Strangely, most people describe overthinking as a negative experience. Yet, when asked if reducing overthinking would be a good thing, many adamantly answer they would not change anything about the way they think.

This standpoint is due to the most robust and potent belief held by overthinkers, namely the fierce conviction that overthinking somehow enhances their thinking, making them think "better".

But in our search for a compelling definition of overthinking, this belief gives us a fascinating hint.

If overthinking makes us think "better", when are we thinking, and when are we overthinking? What is the line between them? How do you differentiate them?

It was the most puzzling question of my interviews.

And what would your answer be as you are reading this? When would you say you are thinking or overthinking?

One interviewee described it metaphorically. In her view, thinking is like warming milk to make hot chocolate, while overthinking is like boiling it.

At a certain point, you have done enough thinking. In other words, the milk is hot, and you should take it off the heat. Overthinking makes a mess of a situation, just like overheating milk makes a mess of the kitchen when the pot boils over.

Surprisingly, when asked about the difference between thinking and overthinking, no two people came up with the same explanation. Some could not even answer the question.

Differentiating thinking and overthinking is confusing.

This is not something we are in the habit of asking ourselves. The various definitions of thinking are as ambiguous and vague as the ones of overthinking. For instance, is "thinking" a conscious process? Or can it also be unconscious? Is "thinking" the opposite of "feeling"?

Given our inability to precisely define "thinking" and "overthinking", the line between the two notions is incredibly blurry.

Nevertheless, one consistent finding emerged throughout my research: we think (and overthink) about things we care deeply about. These can be segmented into three categories: control, competence and connection.

Control refers to the ability to make our own choices, be in the driver's seat and have the freedom to decide. Competence refers to the ability to demonstrate aptitudes and skills. Lastly, connection refers to the ability to cooperate, bond and belong with others.

These elements are the basic psychological needs that must be satisfied to ensure our wellbeing.

This finding echoes the self-determination theory developed by psychologists Deci and Ryan in the 80s[3], which more than 100 studies have since validated.

So, these three categories inform where we direct our attention and, consequently, what we think about most. They form the foundation from which we can establish the differences between thinking and overthinking.

When we overthink, our focus shifts from caring for the triad "control—competence—connection" to fixating on the triad "perfection—completion—validation". We become self-absorbed with and consumed by attaining these things.

Overthinking is Enhancing my Thinking

To be in control, we feel the urge to hide our weaknesses and be irreproachable at all costs. We expect perfection.

To demonstrate our competence, we must come up with fool-proof and fail-safe solutions and finish all the tasks set out before us, no matter what. We accumulate completion.

To feel connected to others, we seek constant praise or special attention for what we do and who we are. We revere validation.

Throughout the following three chapters, we will examine the differences between the two triads, defining a more precise delineation between thinking and overthinking as we go along.

Doing so will enable us to dive into the first myth of overthinking.

We will demonstrate why and how overthinking is actually doing a disservice to our thinking instead of enhancing it. And as we explore the different categories, you will also be given tools and techniques to manage your overthinking better.

Chapter 1

Finding The Tipping Point Of Excellence

"Perfect is a dream that you wake up from and spend forever trying to remember."

Joseph Eastwood

Finding The Tipping Point Of Excellence

Victoria has decided to take a trip to Thailand for seven days. She is frantic with excitement and rushes to her local library to borrow the three available books on Thailand. She puts in a request for the fourth one that is already out on loan for another week.

Almost every night, she works on her planning and itinerary to ensure she sees and visits as many things as possible. She spends hours online combing over the national tourism office website, then comparing different resorts, local attractions, transport companies. She looks at every transportation fare, hotel rate, admission price, meticulously compiling the information in an Excel spreadsheet.

All this research is quite exhausting but worth it. After all, she just found a little gem of a B&B to stay at, definitely offering the best price to value ratio.

Strikingly, even after she made all her bookings and finished her planning, Victoria simply cannot relax. There is always this little voice in her head wondering if she made the best choices, which keeps her tense and nervous until the day of her departure.

An hour after she lands, she arrives at her accommodation and feels a bit disappointed. It doesn't look as magical as in the pictures.

Fortunately, her phone's filters and colour adjustments do little miracles, so the pictures look simply gorgeous when posted on social media.

As she goes through her jam-packed schedule, jumping from one bus to another, visiting temples and markets, one of her friends comments on her last post: "*Go girl! Bangkok is amazing! Make sure you see Railay Beach. It's the most incredible thing to see in Thailand. You CANNOT miss it!*"

It instantly triggers some anxiety.

Railay Beach was on Victoria's to-do list, but she completely forgot about it. There were so many things to plan and see that it completely slipped her mind. She rushes back to her hotel, opening her laptop to see if she can squeeze it in. Maybe if she shortens a few visits, she can make it.

But no matter how she tries, it's not possible to fit this excursion in her planning. But it's such a pity—the beach looks amazing.

Her holidays aren't finished yet, and she is already planning the next ones. As a result, she ends up coming back more depleted than when she left, somehow disappointed that everything didn't go as she expected.

Maybe she should just stay home next time. That sounds like the best option.

◆◆◆◆◆

What should have been a positive and energising experience for Victoria was utterly ruined by her overthinking. Pushed by her desire to get the best out of her holidays, she tried to be "on top of everything", anticipating and planning her trip down to every last detail.

This exacerbated sense of control became an obsession with obtaining perfection.

This is characteristic of the overthinker persona, the "Maximiser", someone who sets unrealistically high standards of performance, relentlessly striving to attain them while hardly ever experiencing satisfaction[1].

Studies extensively demonstrate that this behaviour is driven by fears, specifically the fear of failure or making mistakes, which are interpreted as losing control[2].

Additionally, when reaching perfection is needed to get validation from others, Maximisers can also be subject to the fear of missing out (FOMO). They are afraid of not making the best choice when there are multiple options, which leads to feeling regretful even before the choice is made[3].

Worse, they can still experience regret after making their decision, even if they believe they made the "best" choice, simply because they had to forfeit the other opportunities. An example would be to have to choose between going on a date or to a friend's gathering. Even if they enjoy their lovely evening, they might still be torn apart about the option they didn't choose.

Many go to great lengths to counter this fear and attempt to reach their performance standard.

We often rely on analytical thinking to identify and define problems, extract useful information and find solutions. But unfortunately, when we aim to cover all angles and choose the "best" alternative, we end up doing an excessive amount of analytical thinking.

In fact, we do it so much that we are overthinking.

And this excess of analytical thinking is due to misunderstanding the value of information.

Value of information analysis is a quantitative and computation-heavy method that is often used to improve corporates' and government bodies' decision-making. Although it is effective in some specific professional settings, I will present a more pragmatic and simplistic version we can all use in our daily life. Subsequently, the value of information will refer to the benefits it offers minus the costs to acquire it. A positive value is given if the benefits outweigh the costs, and a negative value if the costs outweigh the benefits.

Here is an example of how the value of information can be used. Victoria took out four books on Thailand from the library. The cost of acquiring this information was going to the library, borrowing the books, reading them and eventually bringing them back.

The first book certainly taught her a lot about what to do in Thailand, so the benefits outweighed the costs. The value of information is positive, which means it was useful to read the book.

But by the time she had read the fourth book, she probably didn't learn much. In this case, the value of information is negative, indicating she could have avoided this activity and done something more valuable with her time and energy.

Now, we can define three core rules that will enable us to efficiently (and without any mathematical calculations) evaluate the value of information.

- Firstly, the value of information increases with use.
- Secondly, more information is not always better.
- Lastly, the value of information decreases over time.

Let's delve into the first rule.

When we consider objects like a car, a computer or a surfboard, we know that the more we use them, the more they wear out and the less valuable they become. For instance, as soon as we drive our new car out of the dealership parking lot, insurers will decrease its value by 10–15%. But information is different from these standard objects.

The more you use the information, the higher its value becomes.

As a kid, I remember my dad having a map of France in the car. There was no mobile phone yet, even less a smartphone with interactive maps and GPS. So when you wanted to find your way, you consulted the bulky book with all the roads of France, from the major highways to the hidden trails. If the map book is never used and stays hidden under a front seat, it has no value. But if you use it for every trip, it gives you value from the information you gain each time.

Similarly, if we already know that new information will not change our mind or course of action, then it serves no purpose to acquire it. If we don't use the information to confirm or refute our thinking and influence what we will decide to do (or not do) next, it provides no benefit.

Information we won't use is actually worse than worthless because, in addition to delivering no benefits, there are costs associated with its acquisition. It's like buying apricots when you have decided to bake an apple pie. Sure, apricots are tasty fruits, but there is simply no point purchasing them for our recipe.

So, if we don't use information, it has a negative value, which leads us to the second value of information rule: more is not always better.

In 2012, a picture went viral of a possum that had broken into an Australian bakery and binged on pastries[4].

The poor animal was photographed lying belly-up in a cardboard box full of pastries. He looked both defeated and sated. He had clearly eaten more than he should have and could not move an inch.

Although it seems funny at first, it highlights a survival behaviour that has been profoundly ingrained in us for aeons. It comes from the reptilian part of our brain, the cortico-basal ganglia[5]. It rewards some of our behaviours with a release of dopamine and gives us the impulse to repeat this behaviour. In the absence of more advanced cognitive functions that recognise satiety, or the ability to predict how bad we will feel, there is nothing to stop us from eating.

Act Before You overThink

We want more and don't want to stop.

From an evolutionary point of view, it makes sense. In ancient times, food was scarce and not readily available. When our ancestors had access to it, the idea was to eat as much as physically possible to stock up for the days to come when food would not be as plentiful.

We adopt the exact same behaviour with information.

So why do we always want more information? Just like with food, information also offered a precious advantage for survival. Finding and recognising footprints that indicated whether we were in danger was vital. The same applied with recognising and identifying edible berries (and distinguishing them from poisonous ones), and locating fresh water. Actually, any clues about predators, food supply and shelters were extremely precious.

The more information our ancestors had, the higher their chances of surviving.

But none of these signs are easy to pick up on and understand. So, we are programmed to acquire as much information as possible and decipher it afterwards.

For example, when we see a bush moving, it is best to consider the possibility of a lion lurking rather than foolishly ignoring it. We pick up on this danger signal, even if it is likely only the wind rustling the leaves. This behaviour is still in us, passed down from thousands of generations.

However, nowadays, the internet and other innovative technologies bombard us with information that is not essential to our survival. Our attention is grabbed by flashing pop-up ads on websites, roadside billboards or the TV displaying news at the coffee shop as we unconsciously search for vital information. We instinctively adopt the same behaviour as when we were hunting mammoths on the plains, and we end up like the poor possum trapped in its pastry box.

Finding The Tipping Point Of Excellence

Let's put in perspective the unprecedented increase of information we are consuming. From 1990 to 2015, it is estimated that the information load of managers in day-to-day operations quadrupled[6].

In 2012, researchers from the University of California estimated that people absorb 105,000 words a day[7] through emails, television, radio, newspapers, books and social media. Indeed, they did not read every single one of them, but this was the amount that caught their visual or auditory attention. That's an average of 23 words per second, assuming people are awake 12 hours per day.

So we have access to an overwhelming amount of information, but our ability to process it has not changed.

If you are asked how many things can you keep in mind, what would you say? Can you remember a complete phone number? If you arrive at a party and are introduced to a dozen people, each of them telling you their first name, would you be able to remember them all?

It turns out that our processing memory is limited. A famous study conducted more than half a century ago by psychologist George Miller demonstrated that the maximum amount of information we could keep under conscious scrutiny at any given time was about seven things (such as names), plus or minus two[8].

Researchers later argued this number, suggesting it depends on several other factors, such as the complexity of the task or the amount of training we have. In particular, they demonstrated that we could remember more than 80 digits[9] with proper practice.

Still, whether we can handle more than seven distinct elements or not, there is a threshold above which we are not able to process the information and integrate it into our decision-making process.

Past this point, we are in a state of saturation known as information overload.

For instance, this happens in chess with the notion of combinatorial explosion. When you try to foresee the different moves your opponent could make during their next turn, the number is quite limited (especially if you focus only on the viable ones). But as you go further into the predictions, like which piece she could be moving in five turns from now, the possible combinations of moves increase dramatically, making it harder and harder to incorporate them into your game strategy.

The combinatorial explosion also affects real-life problems like planning for our holidays. Increasing the number of possible combinations of inputs and constraints makes it harder and harder to decide what to do.

Consequently, the accumulated value of information decreases past a certain threshold. Since any new information will overload our brains, and information we don't use is irrelevant, accumulating information brings us negative returns.

The accumulated value of information follows an inverted U-curve function[10], similar to the microeconomic principle, the "Law of Diminishing Returns".

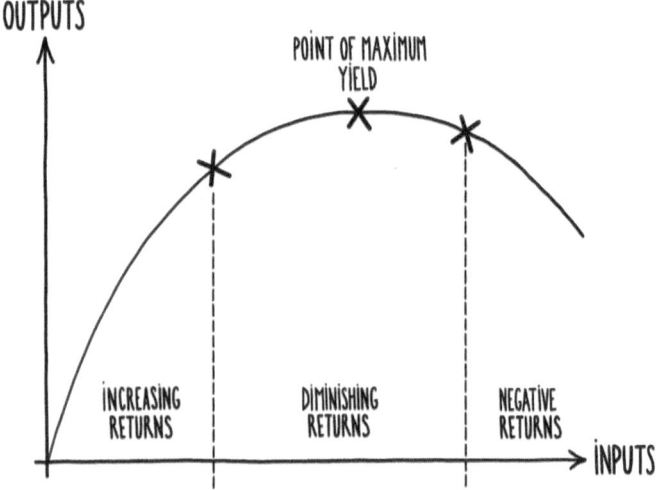

Finding The Tipping Point Of Excellence

This graph shows there is a certain amount of information that will give us the best ratio between the effort to acquire and process the information and the quality of the outputs.

It is like an investigator solving a crime. First, he must acquire evidence to build his case and prove the guilt of a suspect beyond a reasonable doubt. But once this threshold is exceeded, additional information such as what the suspect ate for breakfast two weeks ago and whether he bought his mother a Christmas gift becomes extraneous.

More is not better. More information will not give us a better outcome.

And there is an underlying notion to this balance between the resources spent to acquire information and the outcomes they generate. It is encapsulated by the third rule, which states that the value of information decreases over time. And while it is probably the most obvious rule, it also seems to be the one we are the most oblivious to.

One of the best examples of this contradiction is found in spy movies. After all, who can say they have never fantasised about being a secret agent? In *Atomic Blonde*, the hypnotising Charlize Theron plays an MI6 agent during the Cold War. She is sent to Berlin and fights KGB agents to retrieve The List, a micro-film containing intelligent agents' names and true identities. Even if it is predictable, I profoundly enjoyed the movie using a typical trope for a spy story: some secret agent turned against his agency and country, stealing classified documents and bargaining them against asylum or a tremendous amount of money.

But how long would this information be valuable? Would the classified documents still hold value 10 years after being stolen? What about two years? Or even six months? Nowadays, it's a standard security practice to change companies' passwords every three to six months. So imagine what it would be for nuclear codes?

Of course, there are undoubtedly secrets whose values don't diminish over time, for example, knowing who the serial killer Jack the Ripper was who terrorised London in 1888. Or whether the marvellous Hanging

Gardens of Babylon were in fact real, as many ancient texts claim? However, the answers to these enigmas remain singular exceptions to our last rule.

Generally, as the digital marketing expert Gregg Thaler once said: "*Data ages like fish, not wine. It gets worse as it gets older, not better.*"

Lionel spent a considerable amount of time and energy sorting out all the data he had accumulated while searching for a flat to buy.

In a massive Excel spreadsheet, he listed an incredible amount of parameters, ranging from the most obvious, such as its surface area or the number of bedrooms, to a more qualitative one, like whether or not he found it cosy.

But after two months, Lionel decides not to buy—he has another project in mind.

Three years later, he revisits his market analysis. All the flats he listed back then are now sold. Prices also have increased, some areas much more than others. His son Hugo was born two years ago and his initial parameters have changed. His family now longs for a bigger accommodation, with outdoor space.

The consequence? Lionel's spreadsheet has become entirely useless.

This behaviour is typical of Maximiser overthinkers. During interviews, they often described how they compiled a large amount of data to help them make the "best" decision, especially before making any significant purchase, like a flat or a car.

But we must remember that information is perishable. Information has a sell-by date and it holds no value anymore when this date has elapsed.

As a result, these three rules show the trade-off between time and usage to optimise the value of our information. If we spend time acquiring information, we have to consider that the value held by previously acquired information will decrease. So the benefit we get from the latest information has to be higher than the depreciating loss. If it isn't, we are like a kid at the beach, trying to dig a hole close by the sea. Every three scoops, a wave comes in, refilling the hole.

As we focus on achieving perfection and making the best decision, we aim to acquire as much information as possible to eliminate uncertainty and avoid being wrong. But due to the inherent nature of the value of information, it is simply impossible. When we overthink, using our analytical abilities excessively, we are like the little kid at the beach, digging too close to the sea. An excess of analytical thinking is incredibly counter-productive.

Overthinking the data doesn't protect us from failure or making mistakes.

As a thought experiment, if it were possible to never fail, would it really benefit us? If our favourite sports team could never lose, would we still be entertained watching them? If skills, experience and luck were irrelevant because we could never lose a board game, would we still enjoy it? Would others even bother playing with us?

We get a different feeling when extending this idea to our career and relationships. We care more deeply about these areas of our lives and don't want them to meet failure. But to quote the American actress Ilha Chase: "*The only people who never fail are those who never try.*" If we never encounter setbacks, it simply means that nothing is happening. The fact is that no matter how much we analyse and overthink, we cannot shelter ourselves and be fully protected from failures or mistakes. So it is primordial to establish a new perception of these events.

Act Before You overThink

We are not diminished by failure; we are offered an opportunity to rise with it.

Failures and mistakes are like vaccines. We fear the needle and dread the moment we will be pricked. But the same way as vaccines strengthen our physical immune system by exposing it to a weakened or inactive subpart of a pathogen, failures and mistakes can build up our psychological immune system. They offer the opportunity to improve our resilience and to grow.

We might not have control over how much a vaccine's side effects and failure will impact us, but we can control how we let them define us. We have control over the narrative that surrounds the event. We decide if this is happening "to us" or "for us". Shifting from "to us" to "for us" is a choice—the choice to reframe failures and mistakes as a lesson rather than retribution.

Psychologists called this notion "cognitive reappraisal": the act of reinterpreting a situation to alter its meaning and change its emotional impact[11].

It is important to understand that cognitive reappraisal doesn't mean we deny or shut down our negative emotions and thoughts. It is not some kind of forced positivity but rather a genuine exercise to reframe an event constructively. This is by no means easy, especially when we are new to this practice.

When I struggle to find the silver lining in my failures and mistakes, I like to remind myself of the adage "bad decisions make good stories". It tells me that even if I cannot see the bright side immediately, it will come eventually.

More than a decade ago, I missed my return flight from Shanghai to Marseille. I arrived at the Chinese airport having spent my very last renminbis. I had also disabled my local SIM card and its associated phone account. I could not find my flight on any dashboard, so I went to the airline company counter to ask what was happening. They then told me that I had mixed up the departure time. I got confused by the "a.m." (ante meridiem) and "p.m." (post meridiem) times. Reading 12:05 a.m. on the 27th on my ticket, I understood my flight was on the night of the 27th to the 28th when it was instead on the night of the 26th to the 27th.

Huge mistake!

Needless to say, I was not seeing the upside of this situation at the time. But now, I can laugh about it. I gained a "good story". Plus, I can tell you that I have never missed a flight since then!

To help ourselves with the cognitive reappraisal technique, we can ask ourselves if there are (or will be) any positive outcomes that result from our failures or mistakes? In which ways are we better off now? What did we learn, and how can we use these insights in the future? Is there anything we can be grateful for?

As Victoria remembers her holidays, she still feels upset. She sits on her sofa, a hot cup of green tea in her hands, and starts reflecting.

If she was to do it all over again, would she do anything differently? Of course, she would not forget about Railay Beach.

She wishes she had never seen her friend's comment on her picture.

Maybe next time she goes away, she should just turn off her social media. She smirks at the idea of going on a "social media diet" and decides to look again at her vacation photographs.

As she ends on the one where a monkey tries to steal her bag at the beach, she thinks to herself: "*Everything was far from perfect, but what an experience!*"

Key Takeaways

- An exacerbated care for control turns into a fixation for perfection.
- It leads to overthinking, using an excess of analytical thinking.
- This behaviour links with the Maximiser persona and is driven by fear of failure, especially if interpreted as losing control.
- Excess of analytical thinking is due to misunderstanding the three rules of the value of information.
- Rule 1: The value of information increases with use.
- Rule 2: More information is not always better.
- Rule 3: The value of information decreases over time.
- Due to the nature of the value of information, an excess of analytical thinking is counter-productive.
- Overthinking, through an accumulation of data, doesn't protect us from failure.
- Failure doesn't diminish us. Instead, it offers an opportunity to rise.

How-To

To ensure you are not doing analytical thinking in excess, you can ask yourself the following questions:
- Will I use this information or data for my upcoming decision?
- Is this information redundant or overlapping with another one?
- Am I waiting for too long to make up my mind?

Overthinking can be triggered by the fear of failure and losing control. To fight it, we can use the "cognitive reappraisal" technique.
- This is the act of reinterpreting an event to alter its meaning and change its emotional impact.
- It requires changing our mindset to perceive the situations we encounter as happening "for us", rather than "to us".
- It should not be forced positivity, forcing us to deny or shut down our negative emotions and thoughts.
- Instead, it requires constructively reframing the event, highlighting possible positive outcomes. How can it benefit us? What can we learn?
- And remember: "Bad decisions make good stories."

To go further, visit lisonmage.com website or directly scan the QR code. You will find additional resources, including downloadable documents, exercises and videos, to help you *Act Before You overThink*.

Chapter 2

Removing the Resolution Blindfold

"We don't see things as they are, we see them as we are."
Anaïs Nin

Removing the Resolution Blindfold

Dana lets out a long sigh of frustration as she gets into bed. Nothing went as planned today. She was constantly being interrupted and unable to focus. As a result, she did not do what was scheduled and got sidetracked.

Dana is feeling tense and irritated. She should have done more. She certainly wasn't productive enough today. There is a sentiment of shame and guilt she cannot shake. "*What's wrong with me? Why can't I get these things done as planned?*"

And there is a business presentation for a critical customer which is not progressing as she expected. She exchanged many emails throughout the day but didn't get it finished.

Somehow, she cannot stop thinking about the project at night and what's coming next. It's getting under her skin. It's like a rash you cannot stop scratching. She just cannot sleep. She keeps rolling around in her bed or struggling to stay still, but she always ends up staring lethargically at the ceiling, thinking of the presentation.

No matter how hard she tries, her brain won't turn off. Thoughts keep coming as she runs through many scenarios with countless hypotheses. It's going in all directions.

Dana anxiously looks at her alarm clock, calculating how many hours are left before she has to get up and start the day. It's already two in the morning, and she hasn't slept a wink. She has to get up at six o'clock sharp. If a proverbial sandman were to make her fall asleep magically, that would still only be four hours of sleep. She will be in agony tomorrow, gulping down coffee to stay awake.

But sleep doesn't come; she cannot stop thinking about the project.

So she gets up silently, walking warily in the dark to the kitchen table, and opens her laptop, determined to finish the damned presentation.

Act Before You overThink

At first, this behaviour was occasional, so Dana didn't mind it. But then, a few nights every year turned into a few nights every month. And it kept on escalating. Now, she is up working almost every night.

Unfortunately for Dana and so many others, there is always something unfinished, always something in our minds that prevents us from sleeping peacefully.

This inability to rest and put our minds at ease is rooted in an obsession about completion.

It is like our brain is an internet browser opening new tabs for every task we have to complete, consuming a bit of our mental bandwidth. Like: "*Do not forget to buy milk on the way back from work.*"

Closing the tab by completing the task frees our minds and makes us feel better. But there are more complex tasks, like a project, which might open dozens of tabs at a time, monopolising our mental resources. It becomes the only thing we can think about. And this is quite uncomfortable, so we want to close the tabs as quickly as possible to free up mental space and unclutter our minds.

This creates an urge to solve in order to get closure.

Psychologist Maria Ovsiankina studied this behaviour. She demonstrated that when a task is interrupted or simply unfinished, it will cause intrusive thoughts, pushing us to complete the job[1]. We fail to detach from the unfinished tasks, leading to an inability to relax and, ultimately, sleepless nights[2].

These findings are even more relevant nowadays with the abundance of reminders of the work we haven't completed, such as email notifications. But where does this obsession for completion come from?

This behaviour can be explained by the association we draw between competence and completion.

Basically, we are misinterpreting what competence is. Competence refers to our ability to carry out a task successfully. It answers the question: "*Do we have the skillset?*" Whereas completion refers to the result of carrying out a task. It is the result of our competence. Thus, it is easy to develop the mental shortcut whereby if we complete tasks, we are displaying our competence.

This association becomes detrimental when completion is constantly required to validate our belief that we are competent. Most often, an obsession with completion to prove our competence is driven by fear.

It can be linked to the imposter syndrome, which is the fear of being exposed as a fraud. This psychological pattern was first introduced and discussed by psychologist Suzanne Imes and Pauline Clance in the 70s. Individuals suffering from imposterism will keep doubting their competence no matter how many previous accomplishments they have showcasing their skills and talents[3]. And it can happen to anyone, no matter how much "success" they experience.

Michelle Obama is an accomplished attorney and an author and served two mandates as the first lady of the USA. Yet, in a *BBC News* interview, she said she was still experiencing imposter syndrome[4].

Similarly, in an amusing TED Talk[5], Mike Cannon-Brookes, the founder of the tech company Atlassian, which was worth 26 billion dollars as of 2019, explained how he was and still is affected by imposter syndrome.

When we experience imposter syndrome, we can fall into a cycle where we cannot internalise our previous successes and therefore do not develop trust or confidence in our ability to perform. We remain fearful that we might fail at the next attempt, which will blow our cover and expose us as a fraud.

Completion only offers temporary relief that quickly fades. It is never "enough"; we can never prove ourselves, and we must perpetually do more.

When we finish a business presentation at four o'clock in the morning, we close some tabs in our mind, thinking: "*At least it's done. The ball is in their court now.*" It also satisfies our need for completion, sustaining our belief in our competence.

This is a common trait with the overthinker persona the "Finisher", whereby completion sustains the belief of worthiness. They use a typical thought pattern such as, "*If I complete this presentation, I am competent, and therefore I am worthy to my co-workers and the company*", which is triggered by a need for closure.

If you find yourself having an irresistible urge to finish something, to the point that it is taking all your mental space, it could indicate you are getting into overthinking mode. And it truly kicks in when the task is difficult and you struggle to complete it quickly.

Removing the Resolution Blindfold

When we focus on finding a solution to reach completion, we leverage our convergent thinking ability. Namely, we aggregate information and concentrate on coming up with a unique solution that would answer our problem in the best way possible.

But if we struggle to achieve completion, we can easily trigger our overthinking, which will express itself as repetitive thoughts that are narrowly focused on the issue. In this state, we suffer from an excess of convergent thinking, which is detrimental to our ability to solve problems.

There are two reasons why an excess of convergent thinking negatively affects our competence and problem-solving capabilities.

First, it impairs our creative thinking. This sort of overthinking deteriorates our ability to make unconventional connections to develop new possibilities or ways to solve a problem.

Secondly, it also degrades our critical thinking, which is our ability to objectively evaluate, like looking at our reasoning with detachment, almost from a third-person point of view.

So what happens when we lose touch with our creativity? With an excess of convergent thinking, our focus creates a tunnel vision. Like a horse wearing blinkers, we can only see one way forward. We create our blind spots with our selective attention.

In a famous study, participants watched tapes of two basketball teams. One team was wearing white jerseys and the other black ones. Each team had a ball and was passing it around to teammates.

The researchers asked the viewers to focus on the team wearing white jerseys and to count the number of passes they were making. After a few minutes, the video stopped, and most participants could give the number of passes performed.

But the researchers also asked them if they noticed anything peculiar or ordinary while watching the video. 50% of them said they didn't[6].

As improbable as it may sound, what they had missed was a person disguised as a gorilla walking and dancing on the court.

When we excessively focus on one thing, we intentionally blind ourselves from other elements.

This is a mental effect prodigiously well exploited by one profession: magicians! When performing, they focus the audience's attention on something specific. Like their right hand, by waving it, moving a colourful piece of clothing or simply holding a deck of cards. This is called misdirection. And by doing it, they prevent us from looking elsewhere and spotting how their trick is executed.

But misdirections can be deadly.

The AAA Foundation for Traffic Safety stated that nearly 350,000 accidents, out of which 348 were fatal, occurred in 2016 in the United States due to the driver's failure to check their blind spot[7]. Of course, not all misdirections are as dire as a car accident. However, it underlines that our need for cognitive closure when performing a task reduces our sensitivity to alternative hypotheses[8]. Therefore, we are less likely to look at the information that contradicts our opinion, creating single-mindedness.

Overthinkers can spend days going over the same data in their head, trying to make it fit together, to make them converge to a valid solution without actually doing so. It causes a dreadful loop, where the less we are able to complete a task, the more we focus on it and the more we are blind to possible solutions.

For example, if we haven't found the solution to our problem, the reason could simply be that we are not using the right tools. If we are trying to win a tennis game, playing with a hockey cross is not going to cut it.

And this ties in with the misconception that the more time we spend on a task, the higher the chance we will come up with a "eureka" moment, a light bulb of creativity. So we focus and only use our convergent thinking.

But convergent thinking alone won't work. To think creatively, we need two kinds of tools. Convergent thinking must be paired with divergent thinking. The latter requires opening up to different possibilities, exploring different ideas, some that might not even be related to our initial problem.

Suppose our printer refuses to print our document (as is often the case) and is making weird beeping noises. We give the device a death glare because we want the paper printed, and we want it now! It is tempting to click a few more times on the printer icon to ensure our request has been sent correctly. We could interpret this behaviour as an excess of convergent thinking. Still, this is unlikely to work out (except if the goal is to make the poor machine squeal more).

Instead, we should focus on what the root cause of this dysfunction could be, meaning using some divergent thinking. For instance, we first consider the possibility of a paper or ink issue. And shortly after, we apply our convergent thinking, checking if there is any paper in the tray or if a page is jammed in the machine, then looking at the ink level indicators and maybe restarting the device. In the end, this combination of both types of thinking enables us to find a solution.

It then is no wonder that when studying the psychological base for an inventor's success, researchers found that deliberately controlling the use of divergent and convergent thinking is a key ability[9].

Unfortunately, overthinking prevents divergent thinking.

When we ruminate, we impair our ability to retrieve information we deem irrelevant[10]. Fundamentally, we are unable to think outside the box. We have our blinders on and just look at the road ahead, unable to see the landscape on either side. And this gets even worse with the urge to finish a task. As completion satisfies us, we seek closure. We want to finish tasks.

And the issue is we believe convergent thinking brings us closer to completion, making us feel good about ourselves. On the contrary, divergent thinking can be seen as driving us away from completion, causing negative emotions like feeling annoyed or disrupted[11]. So, we are unconsciously pushed to disregard it.

Consequently, when we overthink a task we need to complete, we use convergent thinking almost exclusively and undermine our ability to perform divergent thinking.

When we do this, we create blind spots. We miss elements that could help us come up with an innovative solution. Thereby, we end up killing our creative thinking, shrinking our problem-solving mentality and eventually shutting down our ability to complete the task.

Overthinking leads us to the opposite of what we want to achieve.

So, if you catch yourself struggling with a task you cannot complete, you should try to reduce your convergent thinking and leverage divergent thinking.

How do we do this? We need to disengage from the problem. We need to create some distance from it. It could be physical distance, like moving out of your office space and going for a walk in a park. Or mental distance by engaging in other activities.

We need to distract our minds and give us some mental breathing room so that we can start linking thoughts and memories randomly.

Imagine your mind as a dog. Rather than keeping it close and on a short leash at the park, we remove the leash and allow it to explore the surroundings, run in every direction, smell the grass and greet its fellow canine companions.

Neuroscientists call these "incubation" periods, where our brain is not actively engaged in an issue but is also far from inactive. Our mind unconsciously processes information, especially remote associations, which is crucial to divergent thinking[12].

They also demonstrated that dopamine plays an integral part in divergent and creative thinking, which is why when taking a warm shower, we have so many genius thoughts, or we can recall a fact we had forgotten for years[13]. These activities, such as exercising or showering, release dopamine and, in the end, improve our odds of having great ideas.

Stanford University researchers even measured it. They compared the creativity performance of two groups through four different exercises. Throughout the tests, the first group alternated between a seated position and walking at a comfortable pace on a treadmill or through the campus, while the other group was forced to remain seated. Creativity stunningly increased by 81% for the walking participants[14].

And another great way to give us more space and foster remote association of ideas is to have a hobby, like playing an instrument or painting. When researchers from the University of Michigan looked at all the Nobel laureates from 1901 to 2005, they found that scientists who had a regular hobby were more likely to win the prize[15].

On average, laureates were 22 times more likely than a typical scientist to perform or sing. They were also 12 times more likely to write fiction novels or poetry. For instance, Richard Feynman, winner of the 1965 Nobel Prize for physics, was also an enthusiastic drummer and bongo player who performed in different orchestras.

As cliché as it might be, when we feel like we have reached a dead end, we should "take a break". Trying to converge on a solution and using brute force might simply result in overthinking and deplete our strengths.

Instead, we should take a step back and immerse ourselves in a different environment to activate our divergent thinking. Once new ideas and associations have emerged in our consciousness, we can then start looking for a solution again.

This combination of divergent thinking followed by convergent thinking is the source of our creativity. Or, as Albert Einstein put it: "*Creativity is intelligence having fun.*"

Unfortunately, an excess of convergent thinking doesn't only deteriorate our ability to come up with new answers to our problems, it also makes us biased. We lose our objectivity. An excess of convergent thinking impairs our critical thinking.

◆◆◆◆◆

Dana has prepared so much for this meeting. She pulled all-nighters working on the business presentation. Even when she was walking at the beach and during dinner with her family, she could not stop thinking about it. It was always there, running in her mind.

Two days before the business presentation, her manager Georgia arranges a pre-meeting session with two other colleagues. A small committee, far from the dozen people expected at the actual event. The four of them get seated in a quiet meeting room, and Dana starts presenting.

Just a few minutes in, one of her colleagues, Zackary, asks a question. Dana gets annoyed. It's pretty basic stuff; how can he not know this?

She gets easily irritated, and her lack of sleep doesn't help. There is some boiling anger ready to be unleashed, but she tunes it down and just answers dismissively before continuing with her presentation.

Several slides later, Zackary asks a second "stupid" question. Dana is now furious. Is she the only one who has done her homework for this presentation? She is about to reply bluntly when Georgia jumps in and tells Zackary to expand on his remark. As he does, he details an entirely different concept, making quite valid points.

Dana realises that she didn't consider this aspect, which is profoundly valuable. It should have been in her presentation. She is so upset with herself. How could she have missed this?

◆◆◆◆◆

Dana spent so much time working on completing the task that she convinced herself she had the unique solution to the problem. Her solution is singular; this is the one and only way to do it.

Her efforts somehow turned against her. She fell in love with her findings and her method to reach completion and disregarded other possibilities. As a result, she became biased in her judgement and was unable to critically assess her work, creating an absolute truth about it that was not up for debate.

Finishers cannot be wrong in the way they do things because being wrong would mean they didn't reach completion correctly. And if they cannot complete tasks, they are incompetent and therefore worthless. This is a direct consequence of their belief automatically measuring their self-worth based on their ability to complete things and display competence.

For overthinkers, completion also ties in with the perception of one's intelligence. So being wrong also means not being smart enough. But this perception is imprecise. Not knowing another method, a different idea or a new concept doesn't make us less intelligent. It has nothing to do with our cognitive abilities.

Instead, it simply means there are gaps in our knowledge. There are and will always be things we don't know. It is an unalterable law of our world. And yet, this lack of knowledge makes overthinkers feel like fools, like Dana when Zackary explains his second question, opening up a new set of possibilities.

So what if we knew everything? What if we had all the knowledge possible and imaginable? Would it prevent us from being fools?

In the movie *Good Will Hunting*, the main protagonist Will, interpreted by the young Matt Damon, is a genius. Will knows about anything and everything with his photographic memory and insatiable hunger for books. But his past keeps haunting him, preventing him from exploiting his immense potential.

Act Before You overThink

After repeated offences, Will is assigned to see a therapist and meets with Sean, played by Robin Williams. Their first session doesn't go well and ends in a strong clash after Will mocks Sean's deceased wife.

What follows in the next scene they share is one of the most memorable and touching ones of the movie, where both Will and Sean sit on a bench in a park, facing a lake. Sean has a frank conversation with Will, saying that even if the young man knows everything intellectually, he lacks experience. Even if Will knows about Michelangelo, he cannot tell what it smells like in the Sistine Chapel because he has never been. Even if he knows about women, he cannot tell what it is to love and be loved. As Sean ends his speech, Will, usually so volubile and sarcastic, is dead silent. Even with all his knowledge, it appears clear to the viewers who the fool truly is.

This example perfectly illustrates how knowledge doesn't draw the demarcation line between a fool and a genius. Through his life experiences, loss and love, Sean acquired wisdom that no amount of knowledge can replace.

So rather than hiding our lack of knowledge and feeling diminished by it, we should be wiser and embrace it. But what does it mean to be wise?

According to psychologists, the notion of wisdom includes the ability to display intellectual humility, meaning recognising the limits of our knowledge. It also implies recognising uncertainty and change, being open to others' perspectives, broadening contexts and compromising[16].

Wisdom tempers the effects of our overthinking. It reduces our judgement biases and fosters our critical thinking. So one might wonder how to be wiser?

To get some insights, we can look to Nelson Mandela, former president of South Africa, who was widely acclaimed as a wise leader.

One of his habits in meetings was to speak last. This way, the other attendees would feel heard, but most importantly, he would hear out everyone before talking. He would immediately benefit from the different takes on the meeting's topic and the various observations helped him form or enforce his opinion.

If talking last is not always practical or even advisable, the main thing to take away is to show openness. Of course, listening to other opinions doesn't mean we need to incorporate them into our reflection or force us to find a consensus, but shining a light from a different angle might offer an original take on an issue that we can benefit from. Plus, another approach to completing a task does not necessarily diminish or oppose ours.

So to remind ourselves of this last point, we can use the difference some linguists draw between solving and resolving. The former means that we have dealt successfully with something, finding the only way to achieve this result. In comparison, the latter is understood as dealing conclusively with something. It doesn't mean it was the ideal way, but one of the possibilities to achieve the result.

When we face an issue, when we have a task to complete, we are not solving it; we are resolving it.

When we look for a new job, the most common way to approach this is to look on different job boards for open positions and then apply, sending our resume and a motivation letter. But what if a friend offers us another approach? Like attending a networking event where one of the company's HR will be so we can introduce ourselves directly. Should we reject it simply because this is not the way we initially envisioned to complete the task? After all, both methods have pros and cons, but each might resolve the task (being hired), and they are not mutually exclusive.

If we catch ourselves being dismissive or belittling other ideas or solutions than the one we picked, it could indicate that our overthinking is at play. We should remember that there could be more than one way to resolve our issue. Hence, we should give other approaches the benefit of the doubt and assess them impartially, to then be able to rationally decide whether to include or reject them.

◆◆◆◆◆

As Dana gets out of the pre-meeting, Georgia pulls her aside. She tells her she did a great job, even if Zachary had pertinent remarks.

"Don't worry too much about it. There are good inputs you will be able to slot in easily. I am sure he would be happy to give you a hand on this too."

For a few more minutes, she keeps reassuring Dana everything will turn out great but she needs to take some time for herself and have a good night's sleep. After that, she will feel much better getting back at it.

Key Takeaways

- Completion is mistaken for competence and incorrectly used as an absolute criterion to evaluate self-worth.
- Overthinkers commonly experience imposter syndrome, forcing them to always perform as they are afraid of being exposed as a fraud.
- This behaviour links with the Finisher persona and is driven by a fear of failure, especially if interpreted as a sign of incompetence.
- It leads to overthinking, using an excess of convergent thinking.
- It prevents divergent thinking, which is an essential step in the creative process.
- It also impairs our critical thinking, pushing overthinkers to reject solutions that aren't theirs.
- This rejection of other solutions ties with the notion that Finishers cannot be "wrong" because it would mean they haven't completed the task correctly and directly diminishes their sense of worth.
- Consequently, excess of convergent thinking makes us blindsided and biased.
- Overthinking diminishes our problem-solving ability and impoverishes our thinking.

How-To

To help you complete a task, you might have to leverage your divergent thinking. To do so, you can do the following activities:
- Take a break
- Practise a hobby regularly

You have to change your environment or do different physical and mental activities. For example, go outside for a walk, exercise or take a hot shower. It helps create mental distance with the task we are focusing on, unconsciously enabling our mind to make associations between remote concepts and come up with new ideas.

Similarly, when you find yourself rejecting new ideas promoted by others, it could be your overthinking at play. To foster your critical thinking, aim to be wise, more than smart. It requires you to:
- Display intellectual humility, meaning recognising the limits of our knowledge
- Recognise uncertainty and change
- Be open to others' perspectives and broaden contexts
- Compromise

To help, remember you want to resolve and not solve. There is often more than one solution to a problem and your focus is on finding one to deal conclusively with a task.

To go further, visit lisonmage.com website or directly scan the QR code. You will find additional resources, including downloadable documents, exercises and videos, to help you *Act Before You overThink*.

Chapter 3

Mastering Mental Time Travel

"How you love yourself is how you teach others to love you."
Rupi Kaur

Act Before You overThink

Ashan went to a party held by his friend Sharon. She is brilliant, just finishing her Master's in biochemistry. On top of this, she is also beautiful and witty. And one of her preferred activities is snorkelling, like him.

While he thinks of her, Ashan cannot stop smiling, but at the same time, he finds himself becoming terribly nervous. He cannot stop overthinking every text sent. Typing, deleting, retyping every message, carefully considering his choice of words. Ashan keeps on wondering what she will think and how she will react.

He checks his phone every two minutes to see if she has read his message or if there is an answer. And in the meantime, he is constantly thinking about how Sharon will interpret his text. Will she smile and find him funny?

He simply cannot stop thinking about the text messages—to the point that when he has to press the "send" button, he feels lost and has stomach pains.

But one day, she doesn't answer.

Ashan can see the message has been read, but she doesn't write back and is not even typing. Five minutes turn into thirty, still no answer! Maybe she didn't like the last message? He decides to send some emojis to smooth it out.

Nothing.

His last message wasn't even read. What is going on? Did he write something that could have been misinterpreted? He starts frantically re-reading the whole conversation thread in the hopes of understanding what went wrong.

Maybe she is just getting bored with him? Maybe she never found him funny to begin with, and now she doesn't want to pretend anymore? Damn it! He knew it! He should have never sent this message. It was so lame!

He feels so stupid now. If only he had known this before sending the text. He could have asked his friend Matthew. He would have told him. It's so doomed now. So why didn't he ask Matthew?

This spiral of negative thoughts Ashan is experiencing comes from an irrepressible need for validation, a perverted version of connection.

Since the dawn of time, humans have been a social species that seek connection. As we connect with others, we form a more significant entity than our own individuality. It allows us to cooperate when facing challenges, improving our chances of survival. Ultimately, connection is one of the core components that allowed us to evolve from cavemen to spacemen.

When a journalist asked the anthropologist Margaret Mead what she considered to be the earliest sign of civilisation, she didn't give an answer many expected. She could have named some iron tools or primitive art, but she didn't. Instead, she believed that the tipping point to becoming a legitimate society was passed when she discovered a human femur that had been fractured and then solidly healed[1].

Any animal with a broken leg would be as good as dead. It cannot run from danger, get to the river to drink, or hunt. It is impossible for the animal to survive long enough for its bone to heal. So the healed femur was proof that someone must have cared for the injured person at their own expense.

It is the first authentic act of connection.

And so, the evolutionary benefits of connection have been deeply ingrained in our brains. We want to belong to a group. We want to be accepted and loved. We want to feel that we are connected to others.

And this profound longing creates a deep fear of being excluded from the group and abandoned, like the wounded beast left alone in the savannah. To appease this oppressing anguish, we look for signs that we are still part of the group. Instead of feeling connected to others, we fixate on signs of validation. We can go to extreme lengths to get this proof.

Some people change their personality and fake their behaviours if they believe it will help a group better accept them. They become social chameleons, trying to always be the right person in the right place at the right time.

For instance, they will happily take a big bite of Aunt Irma's bland cake, smile and convince everyone in the room they have never tasted better, all to prevent hurting the feelings of their beloved relative.

This social shape-shifting behaviour is typical of the "Performer" overthinking persona. Their fear of abandonment is fuelled by the fear of being different, of not being accepted for who they genuinely are. So they end up playing roles and doing what they think others expect of them, rather than simply being themselves.

When the fear of abandonment comes from the fear of loneliness, which is often characterised by a depressing vision of dying alone, people end up putting the needs of others before their own.

They might even sacrifice their wellbeing to ensure that of others. They are unable to say "no" because they have to please others to ensure they are needed and liked. These people are undoubtedly tied with the overthinking persona, the "Helper".

For instance, if a friend calls them for a drink, they will go no matter what, even after an exhausting day at work, where the only thing they truly want is a hot shower, a nice bowl of soup and then slide into bed.

And these two personas will adopt the same type of overthinking to fulfil their need for validation.

They excessively think about social interactions they have had or will have. They believe this extensive focus on these past and future moments will help adapt their behaviours to ensure they belong and are "good enough" to be part of the group.

And ultimately, this leads overthinkers to become experts at time travelling.

The idea of being able to venture through time has always fascinated humanity. The construct of time dictates our life, from birth to death, so we marvel at the possibility of travelling through it, as it would offer the ability to alter our reality. It would allow us to answer questions such as, "*What would have happened?*" and "*What will happen?*"

Stephen Hawking was a brilliant physicist with a sharp sense of humour. He loved to ponder the possibilities of time travel, to the extent that he hosted a reception party for time travellers, preparing canapes and champagne for his guests. Cleverly, he waited after the event to send the invitations so that people could only attend by travelling back in time. But sadly, no one showed up to share a sip or bite, which might indicate that journeying to the past is not physically possible.

Yet, we are all time travellers!

We all physically travel through time, from the present moment to the next one, at the same pace. But we found another way to travel time and free ourselves from its constraints. We explore it with our minds. We mentally travel through time.

In cognitive science, when we travel back in the past to remember a moment of our life, we use two kinds of memories.

We use our episodic memory to consciously remember an event we experienced as faithfully as possible. For instance, episodic memory is remembering drinking a coffee in the Champs-Élysées two years ago during our holidays in Paris.

And this representation of the past event might be a bit fuzzy, so we enhance it with our semantic memory. This is our ability to remember general facts, like at the end of the Champs-Élysées, there is the Arc de Triomphe, which we could probably see from the coffee terrasse.

This combination of semantic and episodic memories allows us to travel in the past. And we can then use and extrapolate our past experiences to imagine future ones[2]. We can recall and predict, which is one of the most powerful and advanced cognitive functions of the human species.

And there is no doubt that mental time travel, granting the ability to envision the future, improved the survival rate of our ancestors and became a selective advantage[3]. It enables us to forecast, plan and prepare. It fosters our understanding that even if we are not hungry now, we will be in the future, and consequently, we would be better off anticipating.

But mental time travel goes even one step further.

We can travel to an alternative past. We can use our two memory types to modify an event or even create one that never occurred. These plausible but speculative scenarios are called counterfactuals because they define events that are counter to the facts[4]. When we play with these mental simulations, we perform some counterfactual thinking.

You might not know it, but you use your counterfactual thinking quite a lot. For instance, as soon as you ask "What if?", you will trigger it. What if I had done this? What if I had known that? This line of questioning means you are creating counterfactuals.

And it happens even at a young age. When recently having dinner with my grandparents, they shared their recollection of an event that perfectly illustrates counterfactual thinking. I was eight years old, and they had brought me to the local fair. To my great delight, I won a game by fetching three plastic ducks in a water bucket using a tiny plastic fishing rod. I had to choose a prize among many colourful balloons. I decided to take the navy-blue one. They noticed that as soon as I walked away from the stand, I started wondering: what if the green one was better?

Counterfactuals are mostly related to our goals and serve two main functions: an affective one and a preparative one.

When we imagine how things could have been worse, we produce downward counterfactuals. They will appease us and we will feel emotions such as relief, optimism and even gratitude[5].

As my eight-year-old self arrived home, worrying that I didn't choose the right balloon, my granddad picked up on my defeated mood. He gave me a warm look and, with a kind voice, asked me, "*Isn't it great that you got a balloon from the fair? If you had missed the third duck, you wouldn't have won.*" Suddenly, my face lit up. I had won a balloon after all!

Researchers compiled a large dataset of podium photographs from five consecutive Olympic games from 2000 to 2016. For each photo, they use an algorithm to assess the facial expression of both the silver and the bronze medallists. Surprisingly they found that the bronze medallist often seemed happier than the silver one[6].

This finding is partially explained by the fact that some bronze medallists engage in downward counterfactual thinking. They made it to the podium when so many others didn't.

On the other hand, silver medallists compare themselves to gold medallists. As they didn't get the medal they wanted, they cannot help but think about how they could have done better. What if they had accelerated at the last turn? What if they had more time to train? They create upward counterfactuals, which are alternative realities where they would have performed better, winning the top prize. Comparing the current and the invented realities often causes regret and can also evoke emotions such as guilt and shame[7]. So the silver medallists frequently appear far less content than the bronze medallists.

However, these upward counterfactuals are not just there to make us feel bad about a past event. They serve a purpose, even if it works differently from the downward counterfactuals.

In the Disney movie *The Lion King*, Simba, the heir to the throne, blames himself for his father's death. He left his native land years ago in an attempt to hide and forget his guilt. When the monkey Rafiki finally finds him, Simba opens up, explaining that he fears going back and facing his past. Hearing this, the baboon hits him on the head with a stick.

"*What was that for?!*" roars the lion.
"*It doesn't matter! It's in the past,*" says the wise monkey.
"*But it hurts!*" objects Simba, to which Rafiki answers magnificently, offering the lion a life-changing piece of advice.
"*Ah yes, the past can hurt, but the way I see it, you can either run from it or learn from it.*"

Following these words, the monkey attempts to hit the lion once more, but Simba avoids the attack this time, proving that we can learn from our past and progress.

Upward counterfactuals serve a preparative function, highlighting how we can improve our future using our learning from the past.

Unfortunately, wrongly used upward counterfactual thinking can also have disastrous health and social consequences.

Firstly, it is essential to acknowledge that counterfactuals are not perfect simulations. They can be inaccurate as they are constructed using our episodic and semantic memories. What if we remember being on the Champs-Élysées in Paris when instead we mixed it up with the beautiful district of Saint-Germain-des-Prés?

The Innocence Project, a non-profit organisation in the USA, provided a harrowing example of how memories can fail us. From 1989 to 2014, the association successfully overturned 325 convictions using DNA evidence. More than one third of the convicted persons were sentenced to life in prison or the death penalty. And in 72% of these cases, namely 234 of them, the conviction was backed by an incorrect yet genuine eyewitness testimonial[8]. Most often, involuntarily, individuals didn't recall the event correctly, which led to an erroneous judgement.

There is a multitude of factors that can alter our memories. And if they can be imperfect, so can our counterfactuals.

Isabel, Nikola's manager, passed by his desk and asked him to meet her in her office in two hours to discuss something. She didn't tell him what this is all about, so his mind starts running at full speed.

Did she ever call him into her office before? What could she want to talk about? And why do it in her office? Is she about to fire him?

Nikola is pretty sure that when you are summoned like this, it's to be fired. Thinking back on it, she did look agitated when walking through the office this morning. And last week, he embarrassed himself in front of the whole team, mixing up data and coming up with wrong conclusions. He knew it; he should have spent more time working on this. It was not good enough, and Isabel is not the kind of person that settles for mediocrity. He is so done for right now.

Getting caught up in a whirlwind of thoughts, the wait becomes unbearable.

It is finally time, and while walking to Isabel's office, he cannot help but notice his legs shaking and how sweaty his palms are. She welcomes him with a smile and asks him to sit. Nikola thinks this is quite a sadistic way to tell someone they are being sacked.

"Nikola, I think you did a great job over the last quarter, and there is a new managerial position that is opening in Giorgi's department. I believe it would be a great move for your career, and I would be happy to push your application if you want to."

This story is far more common than you might initially think. There are several cognitive distortions and biases at play here.

First, we jump to conclusions, drawing a negative conclusion while missing supporting evidence[9]. Overthinkers are particularly adepts at a derivative called mind reading, where they infer what a person is thinking based on their non-verbal cues. Assuming they could correctly pick up on these signs, they often misinterpret their causes. Isabel might have been worked up as she walked through the office, but is it really because of Nikola? Could she have had a sleepless night? Or an argument with her sister?

Another bias working against us is the spotlight effect. We believe our actions are noticed more than they truly are, as if we were on stage, under a spotlight[10]. It is particularly potent for embarrassing events, where we inaccurately evaluate how much we are being observed. For example, if Nikola had asked his colleagues a week later about his blunder, they would have probably told him they could not remember it.

And so, if our mental simulations can be biased, they can lead to erroneous conclusions. Counterfactuals are not an absolute truth.

The silver medallist might imagine that starting his sprint sooner could have helped him beat his competitor. Yet, there is no certainty this would have happened. What if seeing him accelerate, the future gold medallist would have upped his pace too? What if, by speeding up sooner, the silver medallist would have run out of stamina before crossing the finish line?

Upward counterfactuals hint at what we could have done better, but it is only half of the picture. We still have to test them against our reality.

Unfortunately, overthinkers most often do not implement their ideas and remain stuck in their upward counterfactual thinking. Instead, they extensively focus on engineering how they could have achieved a better result. They constantly repeat the past event in their mind, going over how they should have acted again and again, what they should have said, what they should have understood.

Sadly, the contrast between their current and preferred reality creates anxiety and worries[11]. Researchers from the Department of Psychology and Neuroscience at Duke University demonstrated that the more we simulate a counterfactual, the higher the emotional intensity it evokes[12]. This means that if left unchecked, upward counterfactual thinking can severely deteriorate our mental health, making anxiety snowball into much deeper conditions such as depression.

And to make matters worse, counterfactuals can induce negative emotions, but the contrary is also true. A low mood can trigger our counterfactual thinking. It creates a vicious self-perpetuating cycle, where counterfactual thinking causes negative emotions, leading to more counterfactual thinking and so forth[13].

And at first, this is a pattern that can be hard to notice and even more difficult to overcome.

Ashan had a poor night's sleep. He gets up moody and exhausted, turning on his mobile phone. Still no answer from Sharon. As he remembers sending the last messages, he wonders what would have happened if he had sent something else. Maybe he should not have sent these messages. Just thinking about it again makes him so regretful.

And every time he looks at his phone, it triggers the whole memory, making him feel like he is being stabbed. He feels so powerless. What can he do?

Suddenly, there is a notification ring. He jumps on his mobile, wondering if this is her. Sadly, no, this is just Matthew. Ashan texted him the whole story in the middle of the night. That's insomnia for you. And his answer is quite surprising.

"*You aren't thinking straight. Get out of your man cave and get some fresh air. Want to have a drink after work?*"

Seriously Matt?!

Ashan's reaction is pretty normal, yet Matthew is right when we look at the facts.

An uncontrolled amount of upward counterfactual thinking leads to a tremendous amount of regret, anxiety and worry, directly impacting some of our cognitive functions. We become slower to process information, such as reading, taking notes or doing mathematics[14]. Also, our ability to memorise new material, like our shopping or to-do list, is decreased.

So an excess of counterfactuals impairs cognitive abilities.

Ashan decides to meet Matthew at their favourite pub. Again, he explains to him everything about Sharon and how she is suddenly not answering his text messages. Once Ashan is done, there is a moment of silence while Matthew has another few sips of his drink. Then, he looks at his friend.

"*Maybe you should just call her, no?*"
"*Are you crazy?!*" Ashan says.

Ashan is obviously reacting from a place of fear. The fear of finding out he has been rejected, that the connection he has built with Sharon has been severed. Receiving answers to his text messages were a sign of validation. As soon as they disappeared, it triggered an overthinking loop with an excess of counterfactuals.

So how can we counter this negative thinking pattern?

When we start to go down the rabbit hole and fall into this loop of thoughts, we need to act. The first thing we can do is become aware of our unhelpful thinking. As we observe our brain firing in all directions trying to figure out why, in Nikola's case, we have been called in for a meeting with the boss, or in Ashan's case, we are not getting any answers to our messages, we have to hit the brakes.

Once we notice we are overthinking, our aim should be to minimise anxiety and manage worry. We need to regain our calm. To do so, we can use grounding techniques. This will allow us to rein in our mind, which has become lost while time travelling, and return to the present moment.

Sit or lie down and take deep breaths for a few minutes. The simple act of focusing on breathing from the belly, not from the chest, is in itself grounding. When our breathing does not constrain our diaphragm, and we can fully oxygenate our lungs, it slows our heartbeat, stabilises or lowers our blood pressure, and diminishes anxiety[15].

It is important to note that there are many grounding techniques, and there is one-size-fits-all; people might have different preferences or even find some techniques ineffective for them.

Beyond the breathing exercise, another grounding technique I recommend is the "12-Items". Scan your surroundings and pick one object you see, then think of how you could categorise it and then come up with 11 other objects that could be part of this category.

If you see a chair, what category could it be? An object to sit on? Then ask yourself what other things you could sit on "like the chair you see". For every item listed, keep on asking this same question.

What could you sit on, like the chair you see? A sofa.
What could you sit on, like the chair you see? A stool.
What could you sit on, like the chair you see? A park bench.
Etc.

If the first items come to us quickly, the last ones are more difficult. Try for a few minutes, and if you don't find twelve, this is not a problem. The primary intent is to create a pattern interruption. The technique aims to break the spiralling loop of negative thoughts and emotions by forcing our minds to focus on something different, discarding abstract concepts or ideas and solely thinking about concrete objects.

As we become more grounded, we should restore our composure. Then, we can enter the second step, which requires challenging our overthinking.

♦♦♦♦♦

Matthew admits it might be a big leap, seeing the horrified look on Ashan's face after suggesting he should call Sharon.

"But come on, Ash, you freaking out like this, that's insane. There must be a simple reason why she hasn't texted you back yet. Like maybe she's just really busy, or I don't know, maybe her battery died, or she lost her phone."

♦♦♦♦♦

As you observe your counterfactuals, be the devil's advocate. Look for evidence that proves or supports other possibilities than your initial interpretation.

To do so, we can use the principles of parsimony and simplicity. The principle of parsimony suggests that when presented with multiple hypotheses to solve one issue, we should give preference to the one with the fewest assumptions. The principle of simplicity advances that the simplest explanation is usually the correct one, or as the adage goes—when you hear hoofbeats, think of horses, not zebras. Indeed, both principles are not irrefutable, but they are good rules of thumb when confronting our counterfactuals.

If these two steps are not enough to temper our counterfactual thinking, there is a third one that is more radical. We can dissipate the unknown and gain clarity by asking or doing something again.

Nikola could have knocked on Isabel's office door, then stuck his head in the door and said, "*I'm sorry, you must have told me, but I didn't get what the meeting was for?*" The silver medallist might never know if he would have succeeded by starting his sprint sooner, but he can test his hunch at the next race.

It can be scary or uncomfortable at first, but this is the best way to kill uncertainty and appease our minds.

Authors of horror stories know this exceptionally well. The best way to build up unbearable suspense is to play with our imaginations, limiting what's revealed to a minimum. As soon as we know there is nothing lurking in the gloomy bedroom, fear dissipates and reality sets in. "Asking" or "redoing" is turning on the light in our room, realising there is no thief in our kitchen, but simply our cat jumping on our drying plates. Reality is often far less crazy and frightening than our imagination.

Encouraged by Matthew's input, Ashan decides to send a new text to Sharon, asking if everything is all right on her side.

"Yes! The last two days have been crazy at work. Come over to my place to have a drink and I'll tell you more."

Key Takeaways

- Since the dawn of time, humans have been a social species, seeking and caring for connection.
- We fixate on signs of validation we interpret as proof of connectedness.
- To ensure they are accepted by others, Performer overthinkers change their personality and play roles to conform to what they believe others expect of them.
- Similarly, "Helper" overthinkers place the needs of others before theirs to ensure they are needed and liked.
- These behaviours are triggered by the fear of abandonment and loneliness.
- It leads overthinkers to create counterfactuals, where they constantly revisit past events to imagine what they could have done better.
- The difference between their current and alternative realities causes negative emotions such as regret, anxiety and worry.
- Counterfactuals are based on memories, which can be altered or biassed. Consequently, they are not absolute truth and must be used with caution.
- Excess of counterfactual thinking impairs other cognitive functions.

How-To

When we are caught in a downward spiral of negative thoughts, it is crucial to normalise our emotional state first.
- Bring awareness to your current state, recognising the negative emotions and thoughts you are experiencing and that you might be overthinking.
- Start breathing deeply for a few minutes. They should come from the belly, not the torso.
- Practise grounding techniques, such as the 12-Item technique (more on my website).

Then, we can challenge our negative thoughts.
- As you might be jumping to conclusions, remember you might be reading too much from non-verbal cues, inferring what others think without supporting evidence.
- You can also be subject to the "spotlight effect". This cognitive bias tricks us into believing our actions are observed by others more than they truly are.
- Taking into consideration these two points, be the devil's advocate. Find proofs that back the other possibilities than our initial view.
- To do so, we can use the principle of parsimony, stating that we should prefer the hypothesis with the fewest assumptions.
- We can also use the principle of simplicity, where the simplest explanation is usually the correct one.
- And finally, we can act. We can ask again or redo something to gain clarity and dissipate uncertainty.

To go further, visit lisonmage.com website or directly scan the QR code. You will find additional resources, including downloadable documents, exercises and videos, to help you *Act Before You overThink*.

Conclusion of the First Myth

Throughout this first section, we attempted to define overthinking, giving detailed situational and behavioural examples, but first and foremost, to shed light on what it is not.

Overthinking is not thinking.

Or, if we consider any cognitive ability to be "thinking", then overthinking should be labelled as "maladaptive thinking". Overthinking is not thinking but an excess of thinking.

As we prepare our hot chocolate and realise our boiling milk is overflowing, messing up the entire kitchen, what should we do? Take the pot out of the element or add more milk?

When we excessively care about control, we fixate on perfection instead and expect to achieve something with an excess of analytical thinking. Like a possum storming into a bakery, we binge on information aiming for the "best" decision. We overdose on this unhealthy information diet and obtain subpar results.

Overthinking through an excess of analytical thinking leads to the exact opposite of our objective as it reduces the performance of our analytical thinking.

When we excessively care about competence, we fixate on completion instead. As a result, we set ourselves to accumulate as many finished tasks as possible through an excess of convergent thinking. We become blindsided to other options and biased in our approach.

Overthinking through excess of convergent thinking impairs both our creative and critical thinking, effectively reducing our ability to complete a task and display competence.

When we excessively care about connection, we fixate on validation constantly for external approval. To ensure we will be accepted and loved, we revisit our past through a constant cycle of "what-if" scenarios using counterfactual thinking to excess.

Overthinking through an excess of counterfactual thinking plunges us into a self-perpetuating negative feedback loop, deteriorating our ability to process information and remember things.

The first myth of overthinking should now have been busted. Overthinking is not enhancing our thinking. On the contrary, and the reason is simple: overthinking is an excess of thinking that is detrimental to our mental capabilities.

Second Myth

Overthinking is Inconsequential to Me

If you have already come to terms with the first myth then you have acknowledged that we do not benefit from overthinking but instead suffer from this condition. Have you taken any steps to manage it?

If you haven't, you are not alone.

Even though overthinking is perceived as harmful, it appears through my interviews that there was no sense of urgency to do something about it. Instead, there was a form of acceptance.

When overthinkers evaluate their overthinking behaviour, they consider it to be only a small issue in the big scheme of things, akin to the lightbulb in one of your cupboards being broken. It is not an emergency you have to deal with. This is not as threatening as having a power outage or a broken window right in the middle of the winter season.

Somehow, despite the evidence proving the impacts of overthinking on people's lives, it is relegated to a low priority. There is always something else that needs to be addressed first. And because it is never an urgent task on one's to-do list, it keeps on being carried over week after week.

This leniency is reinforced with the idea that overthinking and its impacts remain stable over time. There is a disastrous consensus among overthinkers that if nothing is done, no improvement will magically manifest, but at the same time, they trust that it won't get worse. The logic is, if overthinkers can bear with the situation now, they will be able to bear it then.

And this reasoning forms the belief that overthinking is inconsequential.

But overthinking does not remain constant. Instead, it evolves, and its lingering effects compound over time. Overthinking is a mental leak, spitting thoughts in excess everywhere. And like a water pipe leaking behind a wall, no matter how small it is at the beginning, it needs to be fixed. It is pernicious as we do not see the impacts immediately. Slowly, we notice there is more humidity in our accommodation. Then, we observe a slight change in colour in some parts of the room. And when we realise we need to take action, it is already too late and now the damage is massive.

And one of the reasons we fail to recognise the true impact of overthinking is due to the lack of awareness of how it can affect us.

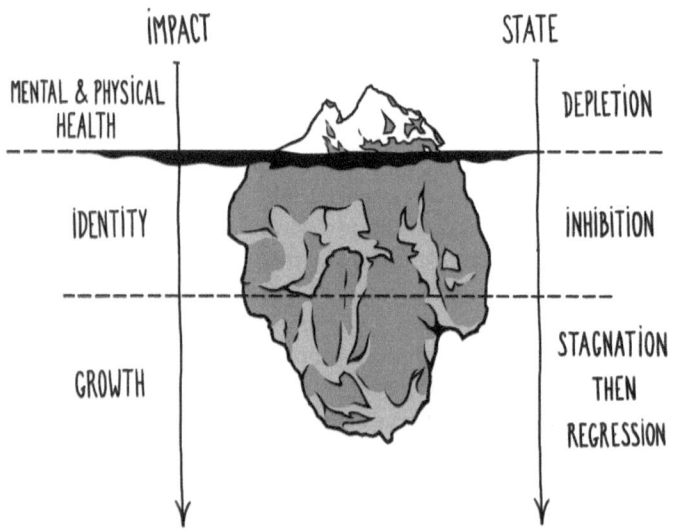

Overthinking is Inconsequential to Me

Overthinking depletes our mental and physical health. Even though overthinkers generally notice this aspect, they are often tempted to neglect it since the symptoms might be, at first, tenuous.

On the other hand, they are oblivious of the impact overthinking has on their identity and growth. Overthinking deceives them, perverting their sense of self and forcing them into a state of inhibition. Overthinking also prevents them from blossoming to their full potential, keeping them in stagnation and creating life-long regrets about their missed opportunities.

Overthinkers are on board a *Titanic* of their own making, cruising carelessly into the ocean, neglecting pack ice. *"It's fine; it's just ice. Nothing that can really affect me."* They don't realise the actual size of their iceberg, which keeps on increasing over time, until the day they collide with it, suffering irremediable damages.

Over the following three chapters, we will explore why we are blind to the different effects of overthinking and their impacts. Contrary to our initial beliefs, it will show how overthinking has terrible consequences on us and why we should reassess it as one of our top priorities to address. And eventually, as we better understand our overthinking, we will be equipped to chip away at the ice.

Chapter 4

Addressing the Elephant in the Room

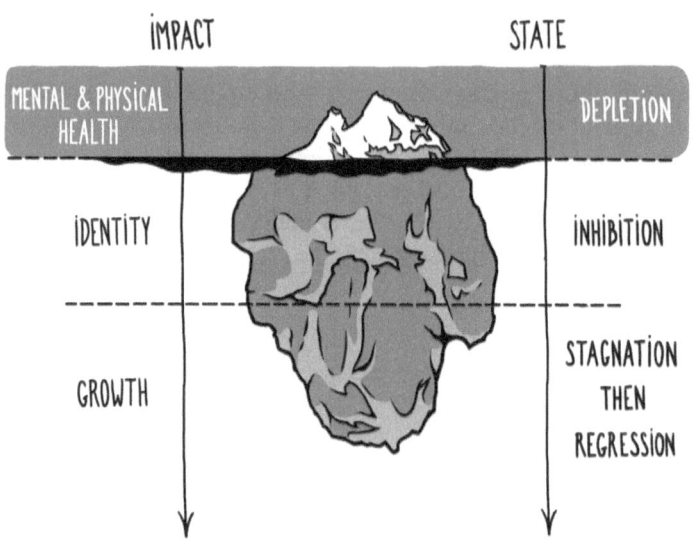

"He who concealeth his disease cannot expect to be cured."
Ethiopian Proverb

Addressing the Elephant in the Room

Since her teens, Jenna has always loved painting watercolours. It is her getaway. She usually sits near a window, with the morning light illuminating her painting canvas. But lately, she faces her easel, brush in hand, but her canvas remains blank. Jenna's mind wanders in all directions, restlessly jumping from one topic to another, and she cannot focus.

◆◆◆◆◆

Shane and his wife decided to trek in a gorgeous national park for an entire afternoon. But every step of the way, all he can think about is work. So much so that he almost doesn't notice the surrounding scenery. Shane cannot turn off his mind, and he cannot enjoy the nature around him, unable to be in the present moment.

◆◆◆◆◆

Yue looks at her phone with anguish. She has to call a recruiter about a new position. She did prepare extensively, but somehow, she just cannot make the leap. Yue's mind is about to explode, running through so many possible conversations, yet she freezes, unable to make her phone call.

◆◆◆◆◆

None of these stories are related, but each shares the same ending. People arrive at the same conclusion: "*No, this is not ideal. But overthinking is not a big deal. I can handle it. It's fine.*"

And you, do you think this is fine?

Should we accept not being able to focus during our hobbies, enjoy the scenery, or make a simple phone call simply because they are mild symptoms of overthinking?

When a child falls and scrapes his knees, we help him get up, clean his wounds and put on a plaster. We know this is not dire; after all, he can still walk, and he will be running again in an hour. Yet, we still dress the wound.

Why should it be any different with our mental health and our overthinking? You might say this is not the same. You can deal with it. After all, it's bearable. But if this mental wound is left unattended, it doesn't heal itself. On the contrary, it worsens and becomes intolerable.

Do you have a box in your flat where you keep old power cables, rubber bands, bolts and screws that appeared out of nowhere but that you cannot bring yourself to throw away? If you don't, you probably know someone who does. The reason this box is there is because "*we never know—it might be useful in the future*". But when was the last time we actually used anything that was in that box? Most probably never.

And the box starts small, one screw there, a cable here. Then it turns into a larger one. We begin adding gifts we dislike, old clothes, university papers, books, etc. The box has now multiplied. It takes up too much space in the apartment so we moved everything into the basement. We added the bikes our kids have outgrown, lava lamps that have gone out of style, board games we don't play and empty pieces of luggage we will never use. Soon, there is no more space in the basement or our closets. It starts invading the living room. Our house looks so much smaller. There are "might-be-useful-one-day" boxes everywhere. It is now oppressive. It is as if we cannot breathe in our home. And the more boxes we pile up, the worse the situation becomes. Do you think this is sustainable?

But this is precisely the same with overthinking. The more we keep all these thoughts in our heads because they might be helpful, the worse we feel.

So, it is essential to look after our mental health to the same extent as we do with our physical health. But we often don't. One of the issues is that we see overthinking as simply an inconvenience, when it should be considered a mental disorder.

According to the American Psychiatric Association, a mental disorder is defined as a health condition characterised by alterations in thinking, emotions or behaviour associated with distress or problems functioning in social activities[1]. And overthinking appears to fall quite easily under this definition.

But for many, even with the realisation that overthinking is a mental disorder, they do not act upon it. Instead, they just live with it. They allow overthinking to add boxes in their mental space until there is no more room available and they are completely boxed in.

In fact, we could say that they are in an abusive relationship with overthinking, which is a ruthless and cunning partner. They ask it if it is okay to go out and it looks disdainfully at them. Then, with a smirk on its face, it wonders out loud if they should really put this dress on. "*Really? I mean, it's quite a bold choice for someone who hasn't been hitting the gym for the last three years ...*" And when they open up about a new position at work, overthinking reminds them, "*Don't waste your time. You don't have the seniority, the experience or the skills. So why would they even consider your profile?*"

Overthinking fuels our inner critic and our negative thoughts. While a moderate amount of self-criticism can increase our self-awareness and foster personal growth, high levels have a disastrous impact on our mental condition. It leaves us in a state of emotional distress, damages our confidence and lowers our resilience in the face of life's challenges[2]. And when we overthink, we generate an excessive amount of thoughts, and our self-criticism intensifies and becomes toxic. So, the question is, why do we allow our overthinking to stay in our lives?

Most often, overthinkers are aware of their overthinking and acknowledge some of the negative impacts overthinking has on them, but they refuse to address the issue. They cannot let go. They cannot leave their abusive partner and refuse to accept the toxicity of their relationship.

"*It's not always bad, you know.*"
"*Things will get better; it didn't mean to hurt me.*"
"*I'm scared of what will happen if I stop overthinking.*"

The main reason for our acceptance is rooted in our first belief that overthinking can be empowering and have an ameliorative function. Somehow, we believe there is more good than bad in our overthinking.

Even as we notice its negative impacts, we want to believe our overthinking is like Professor Severus Snape in the *Harry Potter* saga. Throughout most of the story, he is presented as a villainous person, oppressing the main character and his friends. However, he hid his true colours the whole time and revealed himself as heroic support at the very end. But there is no plot twist with overthinking—it is simply true evil, like the dark mage Voldemort.

Addressing the Elephant in the Room

If we don't hold on to this unhealthy belief, then we would be exposed to a profound contradiction. On the one hand, we overthink, sometimes consciously or even purposely. But on the other hand, we admit that this is something detrimental to our mental health. According to psychologists, recognising this blatant incongruity would create a cognitive dissonance and cause profound mental discomfort and stress[3].

A 2013 study conducted among more than 3,000 adult smokers in Canada, the US, the UK and Australia revealed how they rationalise their habit to prevent cognitive dissonance[4], even if the vast majority acknowledged the disastrous impact smoking has on their health[5]. First, smokers talked about the value of smoking, saying it helps them concentrate better, socialise more easily or simply is a necessary part of their lives. They also reduce the risks associated with smoking, implying that the medical evidence detailing the harmful nature of smoking is exaggerated, that smoking is not riskier than other things people do, or that one will die eventually, so why not enjoy smoking in the meantime.

The last point seems to have the highest level of credibility as it relates to our freedom of choice. Yet, it is terribly nihilist and selfish. If you were to hear a parent say, "*I don't look after my kids. They will die eventually, so what's the point anyway?*", how would you react? You would probably be shocked by such an attitude. But why should it be more acceptable to say we don't mind our self-destructive behaviours because we will die one day? Aren't we hiding from the fact that we are depriving our loved ones of our best selves? Or our future self from a healthy and pleasant life?

Like smokers, overthinkers deny the reality of their conditions. Like the Black Knight from the comedy movie *Monty Python and the Holy Grail* who just lost his arm in a sword fight but insisted, "*This is but a flesh wound.*"

The facts don't lie. An overwhelming abundance of findings demonstrate that overthinking is toxic to our mental health. Overthinking is strongly associated with and can create negative thoughts and emotional states such as sadness, anxiety and worry while exacerbating their intensity and prolonging their duration[6]. Overthinking is also a strong predictor of depression: overthinkers are four times more likely to experience a depressive episode than non-overthinkers![7]

Overall, more than 200 studies have investigated the damages that overthinking has on our mental health, validating its dramatic impact[8]. And the worse thing is that once this behaviour is ignited, it amplifies and multiplies. There is a terrible snowball effect in play, where symptoms start small but keep on growing larger and more serious.

Overthinking also cripples our physical health. For instance, overthinking disrupts our sleep. It takes us longer to fall asleep, plus it also diminishes the quality and duration of our sleep[9].

Additionally, overthinking disrupts our stress response. Scientists noticed that when we overthink a stressful event, our body produces higher levels of cortisol, also called the stress hormone[10]. Cortisol increases the activity levels and neural connections in the part of our brain called the amygdala, which regulates fear.

This often triggers the flight-or-fight response, which is a survival mechanism we inherited from our ancestors when facing danger such as a predator. In this mode, the body prepares itself to face a threat or run away and the heart rate, blood pressure and breathing rate increase[11]. This physiological reaction will also shut down non-essential functions, such as digestion, to divert all energy towards facing a threat.

While this is useful to outrun a lion in the savannah, constant exposure to stress leads to impaired memory, poorer cognition and potentially burnout. And like with negative thoughts, overthinking will prolong a stressful state by slowing cortisol recovery. Namely, our overthinking prevents our cortisol levels from going back to normal[12].

Overthinking can be seen as driving a car in the wrong gear. The motor is running, and apart from the strange noise, everything seems fine. But the car is slowly wearing down until the moment the damage passes a critical threshold and the motor breaks. After that, the car doesn't work anymore, the repair will take a long time and the costs will be massive.

Overthinking depletes us mentally and physically. And as we become fully aware of the toxicity of overthinking, it is natural to want to prevent this behaviour from happening. But before we learn what to do, we first need to learn what not to do.

Firstly, we should not attempt to suppress our negative thoughts.

Jenna returns to her easel and looks at the blank canvas.

As she tries to visualise her painting, she feels intrusive thoughts coming in. Like this awkward moment during dinner with her friends when she mixed up their names. She feels so silly about it that it completely distracts her from her painting. She takes a deep breath, telling herself, now, stop thinking about the dinner and just focus on the canvas.

But the more she pushes back, the less she can think about anything other than her blunder.

Thought suppression is not a way out of overthinking. It is ineffective because it has the opposite effect. Instead of defusing the intrusive thought, it makes it more vivid. So one of the worst things to say to an overthinker is, "*Stop thinking about it.*"

Psychologist and Harvard professor Daniel Wegner called this ironic process theory, also famously nicknamed the polar bear phenomenon[13].

It goes like this.

Pause and try not to think of a polar bear for the next three minutes. That's it. Stay still, perhaps sit, and do not think of a polar bear for the next three minutes or so.

Any success? Science says *"probably not"*. That's the irony of trying to suppress thoughts. If we voluntarily focus our attention on repelling the thought of the polar bear, it backfires and all we can really think of is the animal.

Secondly, we should not attempt to repress our emotions.

Shane and his wife Lara are driving home after their afternoon in the national park. Shane hasn't said a word for a whole hour, simply nodding from time to time as Lara speaks. He is completely lost in his thoughts about work.

His team is behind on the next deliveries. They have been behind for the past six months. They are also way over budget. Anxiety and stress start to chip away at Shane. He works so hard, yet nothing goes his way. He feels like he is slowly losing it.

Lara puts her hand on his leg and asks if everything is all right, breaking him free of his spiralling thoughts.

"Yes … it's nothing. Don't worry."

Expression suppression is a strategy frequently used by men who, when hurt or scared, are told, "You know, big boys don't cry" or to "Man up!", teaching them to repress and hide their emotions[14].

Even if women are conditioned and tend to share more openly their negative affect, such as sadness and worry, they can also use this coping mechanism[15].

In both cases, it feels like being a heated kettle pot. The more we repress our emotions, the more internal pressure builds up. If we are unable to vent, we will blow up.

Although studies found that expressive suppression allows one to modify their behaviour regarding that emotion, it doesn't reduce its intensity[16]. Inherently, the kettle gets hotter, building up pressure, but it looks the same from the outside.

This maladaptive coping mechanism creates a discrepancy between our outer expression and our inner feelings, resulting in a sense of inauthenticity that leads to experiencing more negative affects, ultimately making our overthinking resurface[17].

Lastly, we should avoid toxic positivity.

Yue looks at her phone, still unable to dial the recruiter's number. Instead, she decides to call her mother Mei.

Halfway through her story Mei interrupts her. "*I don't understand you. You should be happy to have a call with this recruiter. Just get over this and call him already.*"

Yue sighs; she knew that's what her mother would say and regrets having called. "*Being scared won't help you, you know. Be positive. Be confident, and you will get the job.*"

Yue hangs up, more distressed and confused than ever.

Toxic positivity is forcing ourselves to think positively and be a "positive" person. It excludes all other negative emotions and instates positivity as the unique emotional state we should experience, no matter the hardships and difficulties we face. It denies an essential part of life and creates shame around feelings such as sadness, anxiety or worry, pushing us to isolate, as we don't want to disclose our emotional state. We wonder, "*What's wrong with me?*", and we start overthinking again.

But negative experiences and emotions are part of what makes us human. We are not defective because we feel. On the contrary!

Responding with a negative emotion to a problematic situation is normal. It's okay not to be okay. Emotions are like teabags. We struggle to control the amount released when first plunged into the cup. The only thing we should do is accept that it is there, and this is all right. However, we can decide when and how to remove the cup's teabag.

There are three steps we should focus on to process our negative emotions: acknowledgement, assessment and adjustment.

There are specific techniques for each of these steps to appease our minds. Note that these techniques are not shortcuts or quick fixes to conquer overthinking, which requires us to get rid of the three false beliefs we hold. Instead, they offer a reliable and effective method to reduce our negative emotions and overthinking.

Addressing the Elephant in the Room

And the first step is to acknowledge we have negative thoughts and emotions.

◆◆◆◆◆

Feeling she just cannot shake the unsettling memory of the dinner with her friends, Jenna starts to explore it more. What is it she feels?

As she was sitting at the dinner table, engaging in conversation, how did it make her feel to mix up her friends' names like that? It was awkward, for sure. But more than that, she felt ashamed. She has known them for more than a decade now. Somehow she is also scared. Will they think she is not a good friend?

Jenna continues with this introspection for a few minutes, scanning and naming her emotions. After that, she feels a bit lighter, and the painful memory seems to slowly lose intensity.

◆◆◆◆◆

Researchers at the Social Cognitive Neuroscience Laboratory of the University of California investigated this specific technique called affect labelling. They measured people's brain activity using functional magnetic resonance imaging (fMRI) when asked to name their emotions and feelings. As a result, they observed a decrease in activity in the amygdala that led to improved emotional regulation[18].

Words have power!

And we can leverage them using the affect labelling technique. As counterintuitive as it might be, when you notice negative thoughts and emotions, you have to welcome them. You can start by just observing them. They are your thoughts, but your thoughts are not (all of) you.

Then, put a name to them, asking, what do I feel in this instant? Don't go into the reasons for your thinking. Refrain from making any causal link.

Act Before You overThink

For the moment, avoid the question, why do I feel this way? Instead, simply and gently ask yourself, what do I feel? Just label your thoughts and the emotions they create within you.

The second step is then to assess. We need to perform an evaluation of our thoughts and emotions. Like the teabag, once plunged in hot water, when do we need to take it out?

◆◆◆◆◆

Shane has arrived home. He unpacks his gear and gets in the shower. As the hot water runs down his body, he slowly relaxes. He is stressed; there is no denying it. But surely there is a balance to find there.

Shane knows challenges motivate him. They also help him bond with his team. So that's not always a bad thing. Yet, he has to find a way to remain motivated by the deadlines and not feel snowed under by them.

◆◆◆◆◆

Shane is indeed onto something. But unfortunately, no matter how we approach situations, there is no escaping negative thoughts and emotions—especially stress. Everyone will experience some stress throughout their lives, but not all stressful situations are equal.

In fact, there are three kinds of stress. First, the good, which is also called eustress[19]. Then there is the bad, which we call stress (some call it acute stress or distress), which can turn ugly over a long period and is then named chronic stress.

Eustress is the stress we feel when responding to a challenge. As our excitement rises, we experience an adrenaline rush and an increase in heart rate[20]. For example, this happens when we ride a roller-coaster or go on a first date. Acute stress is a response to a threat, like an argument with our manager or our child getting sick; it can cause anxiety and a feeling of exhaustion.

Addressing the Elephant in the Room

So, once we recognise that we are experiencing a stressful event, we need to assess its nature. Is it a challenge, or is it a threat? Can it benefit me in some way?

When prepping for competitions, athletes train themselves to harness the benefits of eustress, building up their motivation without letting it affect their performance[21]. Findings suggest athletes who learn to handle eustress develop psychological resilience, meaning the ability to cope with a worrisome event when it arises.

And maybe, the most surprising finding comes from a study that measures the effect of stress on the biological ageing process.

Essentially, researchers observed our body's response to a stressful event, more precisely the level of oxidative damage that occurs, which is a strong indicator of how fast we are ageing. They found that those suffering from chronic stress age more quickly than others. But on the contrary, the people who age the slowest are not the ones who are the least exposed to stress, but the ones with moderate exposure. It means that when we are exposed to a manageable level of stress, we build up physiological resilience[22].

So under the right conditions, we can benefit from a stressful situation. But we have to learn to assess it first. And if we find it to be a threat, we can also use the cognitive reappraisal technique we detailed in Chapter 1 to change the narrative from "things happen to me" into "things happen for me".

For example, our company is restructuring, changing its organisational system. We will be moved to a new team, in a new building. There are rumours that our new manager is seriously incompetent. Is it a threat? Our new team performance will be impacted, and we might not get our annual bonus. But could it be an opportunity to step things up and also learn from a new environment?

What applies to stress management also works for negative emotions. So once you have acknowledged their presence, asking what you feel, you move into the second step, where you can assess these thoughts and feelings, asking why you feel this and is it beneficial to you?

If not, can you reframe it to make it so? Can you change your perspective so that it empowers you instead of depleting you? Sometimes, you can. And sometimes, it is simply not possible. In this case, we go on to the third and last step: adjustment.

◆◆◆◆◆

Yue collapses on her sofa, feeling depleted and lost. She just doesn't know what to do next. Her fear of calling the recruiter is paralysing her. It feels like she is drowning.

Suddenly, the doorbell rings. Who can it be? She gets up, goes to the entrance and opens the door to find a parcel. As she picks it up, she notices the fresh breeze on her face. It is sunny outside and it looks like a nice day.

Yue puts the package inside, then gets her shoes and jacket on to go for a walk. It is warm, and the sky is blue. Today is undeniably a nice day.

◆◆◆◆◆

You might be thinking, is that it? Is going out for a walk the ultimate solution? The answer is a bit of yes and a bit of no.

As we discussed in Chapter 2, changing our environment is a pattern interruption that can lead to the emergence of new ideas to solve ongoing issues. Furthermore, walking regularly, even for a short duration, can be beneficial for our mental and physical health[23].

But walking also ties into a broader concept of restorative activities, which fall under active meditation.

Addressing the Elephant in the Room

Throughout my research, many overthinkers explained that they had tried "passive" meditation with moderate or poor results. They struggled to stay seated, immobile and observe their multitude of thoughts.

Instead of finding peace, they were overwhelmed. They reported feeling like they had been asked to stay still right in the middle of a train station, at the start of the school holidays with people everywhere, talking on their phone, or to their friends, in a hurry, rushing for their train and bumping into each other. Added to this chaos, announcements and music were also constantly running in the background. The noise level in their mind was insufferable.

So instead, an active approach might be more beneficial. This technique aims to move our focus away from our whirlwind thoughts and emotions to allow their intensity to defuse. To do so, we want to channel all our attention into a single point of focus. This requires us to move our attention from our current thoughts, channel them and have a single point of focus.

We want to practise a mindless activity mindfully.

This is the basis of some zen activities, such as sand raking in a Japanese garden. More broadly, we can apply it in some "repetitive" activities that require a high level of focus, such as swimming, archery or dancing but also gardening, calligraphy and singing.

Theatre practitioner Sanford Meisner understood this concept and encapsulated it into his famous eponymous technique.

According to him, repetition exercises were essential to creating an authentic stage performance. In one exercise, actors face each other and repeat a few lines of scripts. They would do this over and over to get in sync with each other and adjust the intensity of their emotions to the right level. The purpose was to help find the emotional truth of the scene, build spontaneity and, more than anything, get the actors out of their heads.

Key Takeaways

- Overthinking is a hindrance that can, over time, turn into a mental disorder if not treated properly.
- Overthinking is like being in an abusive relationship with a ruthless and cunning partner. It fuels our inner critic and negative thoughts.
- Like smokers, to avoid cognitive dissonance, overthinkers increase the benefits and reduce the risks of their harmful behaviour.
- Overthinking is toxic for our mental and physical health.
- Overthinking creates, amplifies and prolongs negative emotional states, such as anxiety, worry and sadness.
- It is also a strong predictor of depression. Overthinkers are four times more likely to experience a depressive episode than non-overthinkers.
- Overthinkers are more prone to experience long periods of acute stress, making them age faster.
- There are three maladaptive coping techniques to avoid when we want to manage overthinking.
- Thought suppression (also known as the polar bear phenomenon) ironically makes the thought more vivid in our minds.
- Expressive suppression hides our emotional reactions but doesn't reduce their intensity and creates a sense of inauthenticity.
- Toxic positivity shames us for experiencing negative emotions, which are normal and an essential part of our humanity.

How-To

To better manage negative thoughts and emotions, we can use the following steps: acknowledgement, assessment and adjustment.

This book presents one coping technique that can be leveraged at each step. Indeed, other ones exist (some are detailed on my website resources) and you might have to try to see which ones are best suited for you.

For acknowledgement:
- You can use the affect labelling technique.
- It requires bringing awareness about what you feel and naming these emotions. Is it fear? Anxiety? Anger?
- Ask yourself what you feel now but refrain from judging yourself and asking why you feel this way, which is part of the second step.

For assessment:
- You need to judge whether the situation is a threat or an opportunity. There could also be a bit of both mixed.
- This evaluation often requires investigating the root cause of your feelings.
- Once you gain clarity, ask yourself if this serves you, if the situation can benefit you.
- If not, you should try to disregard and dismiss it. This is not always possible and it leads us to the last step.

For adjustment:
- You can use active meditation to defuse negative thoughts and emotions.
- Contrary to passive meditation, it requires channelling your complete attention to a simple and repetitive activity.
- We could say we practise a mindless activity mindfully.
- For instance, this activity could be swimming, archery, dancing, gardening, calligraphy or singing.

To go further, visit lisonmage.com website or directly scan the QR code. You will find additional resources, including downloadable documents, exercises and videos, to help you *Act Before You overThink*.

Chapter 5

Dispelling the Lies of the Self

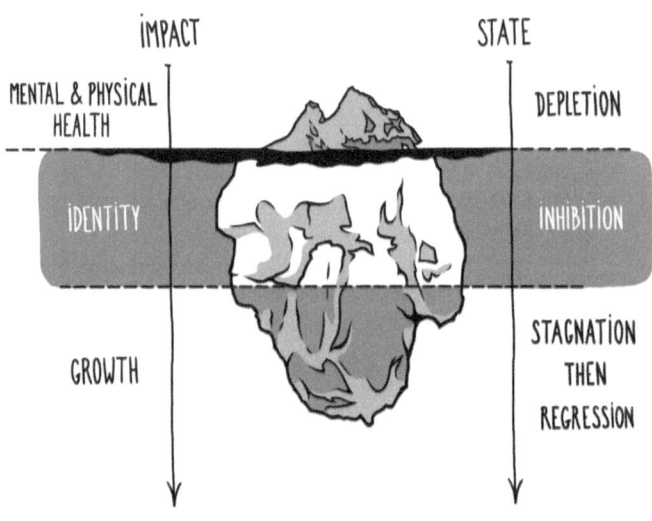

"Hard truths can be dealt with, triumphed over, but lies will destroy your soul."

Patricia Briggs

Dispelling the Lies of the Self

Marcus and his friend Alvaro are seated in a local park, around a chess table, recently installed by the city. It's a peaceful moment to share a coffee and have a battle of the brains. To them, it has become a ritual. Every Wednesday morning, they meet there to catch up and play a few rounds of chess.

Alvaro asks about the promotion Marcus has been talking about for months now.

"Well, I know this is coming, but not right now. It's not the right time. Things are kind of hectic at work, so it's better for me to keep a low profile and wait a bit more."

Alvaro raises one eyebrow, and while moving his knight, he sighs. *"Sure."*

"What do you mean?" asks Marcus. There is an awkward silence until Marcus repeats his question.
"What did you mean by sure? You don't agree, do you?"
"I don't know, Marcus. That's all."

Marcus gets irritated.

"Come on, tell me what you really think!"
"I told you, I don't know!" Alvaro replies.

They return to the game in silence and play a few moves until Marcus furiously says, *"The thing is, people don't understand me. They tell me not to overthink this promotion and just go for it. How do they know that's right for me? They can't know!"*

Marcus stops for a moment, looking at the chessboard, while his friend remains silent.

"I am thinking things through. Yeah, I might be overthinking a bit. But that doesn't change anything, you know."

Another pause and some more moves on the board.

"This is just the way I am. I think a lot and make a move when the time is right. That's all."

◆◆◆◆◆

One of the most ignored aspects of overthinking is how deeply it is embedded in our sense of self, to the point it becomes an indispensable part of our identity.

Overthinkers often told me throughout my research that they didn't want to reduce their overthinking level. Or, if they did want to lower it, they wouldn't reduce it completely (i.e. 0 on the overthinking scale).

They could not let go of their overthinking entirely. When asked why it was so hard for them to fully part ways with overthinking, they answered like Marcus did, saying, "*Because this is who I am.*" Getting rid of overthinking is like losing a piece of themselves, and they simply cannot come to terms with it.

To find out how overthinking became such an essential component of their identity, we have to better understand how we all build our sense of self through narratives.

We all have a narrative, one story, our story. We are all authors, keeping records of the past moments we experienced, imagining and drafting the future ones. And as the author of our own lives, we want to keep our story coherent. We want it to make sense and be purposeful.

Our narrative is the story we tell ourselves about ourselves.

Although it doesn't entirely define who we are as people, our narrative makes our thoughts, emotions and actions congruent[1]. And as we develop our story, we create generalisations about ourselves.

For instance, we joined a tech startup because we are a bit of a geek ourselves. Or we joined a tech startup because we love challenges; we are a go-getter. Or we joined a tech startup because we like small companies where we get to know everyone; we are social. There could be only one or a combination of reasons, which somehow explains our decisions and actions.

These generalisations about ourselves help us keep our story consistent. They help us navigate life's complexity by simplifying some aspects of it. Psychologists define these generalisations as self-schemas, which are mental constructs we develop to characterise our behaviours and ourselves[2]. They will usually revolve around three main aspects: our physical attributes (such as "I am tall"), our interests ("I am a dog-lover") and our personality traits ("I am an analytical person").

And overthinkers, like everyone else, create self-schemas that help define who they are and create a coherent narrative. But more importantly, the self-schemas associated with their overthinking have a positive impact on their story.

In Chapter 4, we saw how overthinking impacts us mentally and physically. Overthinking is depleting us, and we are not our best selves. In these conditions, we can make poor decisions and fail to obtain significant results, which intensifies self-criticism, and generates and prolongs negative emotions, such as anxiety and stress.

In response, overthinkers develop self-schemas to moderate their inner critic and the crippling emotions and thoughts it triggers. Their self-schemas and the narrative they build form a coping mechanism to handle an excessive level of criticism. Therefore, removing one's overthinking behaviour would create discrepancies in their story. Internalised self-schemas would become disjointed and should be questioned to maintain the coherence of their narrative.

It is like the game of Jenga. To play, we first build a tower with 54 wooden blocks, piling them three by three. Then, each player removes one block at a time, which leads the whole structure to become less and less stable. And at one point, if one player causes too much imbalance when removing a block, the entire tower will crumble. For many, their narrative is a Jenga tower and removing overthinking is like removing this last block that makes it fall apart.

Eliminating overthinking exposes all the self-schemas attached to it and threatens the existing narrative structure. Moreover, it would not only leave overthinkers defenceless against their extremely harsh self-criticism, but it would force them to question and reconsider their entire nature.

For instance, if we don't consider and analyse all the data possible to find the right time to act, are we still a patient person? And if this no longer makes us patient, how do we justify the fact that we haven't asked for our promotion yet?

Eradicating overthinking is perceived by overthinkers as a direct attack on their identities. No wonder so many push back against this idea because, *"This is just who we are."*

Furthermore, why risk alienating our self-schemas if they protect us from harsh self-criticism?

University of Glasgow professors led interesting sociological research on drug abuse recovery[3]. They interviewed former drug addicts to understand the role of narratives, namely what they told themselves when trying to overcome their addiction.

They were especially interested in triggers that led to the turning point when they decided they no longer wanted to be addicted. The scientists found that triggers can be a positive or negative experience, such as getting a new job, the birth of their first child, facing prison or severe health complications. When a trigger occurs, the addict reinterprets various elements of their drug use, seeing it in a negative light where before it was something positive. Suddenly, drugs that were seen as "enjoyable, exciting and stimulating" are reframed as "damaging, debilitating and depleting".

The addicts realised that drugs didn't make them confident, powerful or liberated. In fact, they were insecure, powerless or trapped. The false self-schemas they formed when using drugs were shattered once they understood that they were lying to themselves.

Dispelling the Lies of the Self

Overthinkers similarly delude themselves. And one of the keys to recovery for overthinkers lies in understanding how. Throughout the interviews, I observed that the deception happens with the self-schemas overthinkers embrace and incorporate into their narrative.

There are three of them. The first one is "I am attentive". An example of this is when an overthinker meets with someone they have a crush on but don't express their feelings. When their inner critic blames them for remaining silent, they quiet him with, "*I felt her mind was somewhere else. She was worried. This was not the right time to open up. I was putting her needs first.*"

The second self-schema is "I am patient". Overthinkers tell their inner critic, "*I am waiting to allow time for our relationship to grow. I will know when the time is right.*"

The third and last self-schema is "I am realistic". In this case, overthinkers say to their inner critic, "*There is no way I am telling her, she is way out of my league, so realistically what are the odds she likes me back?*"

Now, overthinkers might not have all three self-schemas, but most often, when they are reluctant to let go of their overthinking behaviour, they internalise at least one of these. And the issue is that they are all lies.

They misuse these mental constructs to explain their behaviours and create a coherent and positive story.

- They mistake avoidance for attentiveness.
- They mistake procrastination for patience.
- They mistake resignation for realism.

But why are they distorting things? Why are they deceiving themselves? According to neurologist and founder of psychopathology Sigmund Freud, we engage in self-deception to protect ourselves from the pain and evade the discomfort associated with threatening information[4]. Predominantly, we distort our awareness and lie to ourselves to preserve our psychological health and wellbeing[5].

Avoidance, procrastination and resignation are negative traits, whereas attentiveness, patience and realism are positive. And this is the profound reason why overthinkers are lying to themselves. After all, no one wants to be seen as procrastinating when they could be seen as patient.

But if these maladaptive self-schemas appear to protect us, at least in the short term, they disserve us over time. Author Leo Tolstoy warned us of the consequences of self-deception in one of his most famous novels, *The Death of Ivan Ilyich*.

The protagonist Ivan has just been promoted to the prestigious position of magistrate when he suddenly becomes terminally ill. Bedridden and too weak to work, Ivan doesn't comprehend his terrible fate as he believes he has lived a just and honest life. As it comes to a close, Ivan has an epiphany, realising he lied to himself. He thought, "*I had been going downhill while I imagined I was going up. [...] And now it is all done and there is only death.*"

Dispelling the Lies of the Self

Deceiving ourselves is like betraying life itself, which then gets taken away. In the case of overthinkers, lying to themselves saves them from the immediate pain of the truth. They don't have to face the fact that their overthinking leads them to passive, negative behaviours. They don't have to confront their inhibitions.

Avoidance, procrastination and resignation are behaviours that inhibit us. They promote inaction and maintain the status quo. They hinder our potential and our ability to enjoy and fully experience life.

Consequently, it is essential to learn how to recognise when we are misinterpreting some of our behaviours and how to counter them.

Alvaro met Marcus when they were kids. At first, they didn't like each other much, but they became best friends over time and started this routine of weekly catch-ups a few years ago. Alvaro simply loves being in the park, playing chess. These moments are a real breath of fresh air.

Marcus has been discussing his potential promotion for several months. At first, it sounded like an explanation, but now it seems like more of a rant. Alvaro is tired of listening to the same conversation, so he often tries to change topics but it only offers a respite for a few minutes, and then they are back on the promotion subject.

Sometimes, Alvaro wants to scream, "*Enough is enough! Just go and ask for this damned promotion already! What on earth are you waiting for?*" But he never does. He can tell how much it means to Marcus, and he doesn't want to push him too much.

Over the years, if there is one thing he has learned, it's how pointless it is to push Marcus to make a decision. It would inevitably end up in a clash. And for what? It won't change anything. He is better off listening to his friend and not rocking the boat.

◆◆◆◆◆

Alvaro's fear of conflict and the avoidance it creates is typical of the overthinker persona the "Dreamer". These emotional overthinkers tend to keep their thoughts to themselves to prevent any conflict. Often empathetic, they use their awareness to read the situation and adopt a careful and prudent stance. They often soften their voice, adopt an agreeable attitude and concede a point of contention to ensure the conversation remains peaceful. Even if it also means it becomes dull.

Psychologists define avoidance as a maladaptive coping strategy involving cognitive and behavioural efforts to deny, minimise and avoid dealing directly with a stressful element[6]. Unfortunately, if avoidance offers temporary relief as a coping strategy, it only displaces the stressor in time. As we wait to address it, our source of stress grows and can aggregate with other stressors.

It is as if our issue is an inflatable beach ball. We don't want to see it anymore, so we push the ball under the water. But as time passes, we get tired of trying to hold it there. It becomes harder and harder to maintain the beach ball submerged. As we finally let go, it does not calmly rise to the surface but instead bursts out.

Alvaro thinks he is attentive to his friend's state when he is actually scared of the repercussions he could face if he engages in a difficult discussion. Will he lose these days at the park playing chess if he mentions to Marcus that he is rambling and ranting instead of doing? Rather than taking this risk, Alvaro lies to himself. He believes he is listening and sees himself as attentive, leading him to the obvious conclusion that he should not confront his friend. But in reality, he is avoiding it. He is not addressing the elephant in the room.

If he doesn't voice his concern, is he really the good friend he likes to picture himself as? When we don't speak up, are we enabling certain behaviours? Is it the duty of a friend to offer feedback and highlight blind spots? Indeed, some moments are better suited than others for

Dispelling the Lies of the Self

initiating a serious discussion, but we shouldn't keep on postponing it because we have this never-ending feeling that this is not the right time.

And so, how can we differentiate when we are truly attentive and when we are avoiding a situation?

At first, it is not easy to assess whether or not we are avoiding an issue whilst we are in the middle of an exchange. It requires practice, like building up muscle through repetitive exercise. And when we start a new training, like lifting weights, we don't use the 50 kg dumbbell straight away. Instead, we should begin with lighter weights.

So, if we are unable to evaluate our behaviour in the heat of the moment, we can start by reflecting on it later. We can remember the situation and assess our reactions objectively.

To do this, I suggest taking a piece of paper and, at the top, writing a situation statement, including what happened (and what didn't). Then draw a chart with three columns, from left to right; write "Predictions", "Perceptions" and "Observations" in each column.

Start by completing the first column on the left, "Predictions". Explain what would have happened if you had opened up. Like Alvaro expects Marcus to be upset and not want to play chess anymore.

In the "Perceptions" column, write down what you felt and how you interpreted the situation. For instance, Alvaro felt that Marcus was frustrated and angry when he talked about his promotion.

Finally, in the "Observations" column, write down what you physically saw or heard. For example, Alvaro noticed that Marcus kept his arms closed during the whole discussion and there were long periods of silence.

Then, cover up the "Predictions" and "Perceptions" columns and re-read what you wrote about the situation at the top of the page and the "Observations" column. As you do this, imagine you are reading it to a complete stranger. Would they be able to guess what is written in the two first columns, or would reading them come as a surprise to them? Does what you filled in those two columns require significant assumptions on the stranger's part? Are they missing information to guess the "Predictions" column correctly?

And then, to answer the question, "Was I attentive or avoiding?", we have to complete each column, but in a specific order.

This exercise allows us to perform a realistic assessment, to check if we are interpreting too much out of too little, and it helps us answer the question, "Was I attentive or avoiding?" But if gaining awareness about the true nature of our behaviour is the first essential step, it doesn't make it any easier to act upon it.

When you have to face these moments and have hard conversations, I suggest you take the same approach as Chris Voss, a former lead hostage negotiator for the FBI. Throughout his 24-year career, he worked on more than 150 international hostage cases and built a tremendous reputation as an expert in negotiations. In his book *Never Split The Difference*, he explains one of the biggest misconceptions about negotiations. To Voss, negotiations are not about resolving an issue between two opposing people. Instead, they are a process where two people team up to confront and solve a common issue.

When overcoming avoidance, you should remind the other person(s) and yourselves that you are siding with them. You are on the same team, and you want to help.

Marcus has imagined countless scenarios, mentally rehearsing how he would present his arguments for getting promoted to his manager. He knows the results and successes he would highlight. He investigated who got a similar promotion in the other departments, including their salaries and job duties.

But he is still on the fence. Inside, he is fuming. He knows he should be promoted. He has earned it. But he doesn't want to rush things. His department, and most of the managers, are under pressure from the board to deliver results. If he goes in, he won't be listened to. This is not the right time. There is too much uncertainty, too many unknowns.

In so doing, he quiets the little voice inside him saying he is undeserving and will never be promoted. He knows his time will come. He is a patient person.

Mistaking procrastination for patience is often driven by fear of the unknown, which characterises the overthinking persona the "Observer".

Although Dreamers are closely related to Observers, they differ because Dreamers are emotional overthinkers, whereas Observers are analytical.

For Observers overthinkers, procrastination is triggered by the fear of failure due to uncertainty. They can never be 100% sure things will go according to plan; it appears never to be the right time, so they keep postponing things.

To understand more about this deception, it is interesting to dissect the difference between procrastination and patience. After all, we can wonder, are there any? In both cases, we are not doing. We are not taking action.

But if there is no difference then, when you are waiting at an intersection where all the cars with the priority pass, are you patient or procrastinating?

So the difference between procrastination and patience does not lie in the outcome but in the decision process. Procrastination is triggered externally by fear (for overthinkers), laziness or denial. On the contrary, patience is a decision that comes from within. We internally make a deliberate and confident choice not to act, knowing it is in our best interest.

You might be asking why this distinction matters if, in the end, the result is the same? Without this difference, how do you know you have waited long enough? When is it time to take action? Are you patiently waiting for the "right moment" to ask for your promotion? Are you patiently waiting for the "right moment" to launch your new product? Or are you hiding behind patience because you don't want to act?

Patience is a conscious decision not to act. It is driven by self-discipline. It is a controlled ability to wait as long as the situation requires, no less and no more.

Well-known actor and martial artist Bruce Lee explains patience as "*not passive; on the contrary, it is concentrated strength.*" It ties in with a profound Taoism philosophical concept named Wu-Wei which could be translated as "actionless action" or "doing without doing". It requires bringing awareness to the situation and deciding the best course of action, which is sometimes actively not doing something.

So, patience is an empowering skill we choose to use, whereas procrastination is a reaction to external emotions like fear. And as we understand this opposition better, we can more easily answer the reflective question, "Am I patient or procrastinating?"

◆◆◆◆◆

The news came two days ago, but Marcus is still processing it. The company is restructuring; some people were made redundant, and there won't be any promotions until further notice. Everything is "frozen".

He wonders if he should have asked a few months ago when he had the chance. Now his shot at being promoted is gone, and he doesn't know when the opportunity will present itself again.

Dispelling the Lies of the Self

His phone rings; it's his elder sister Adele calling. Their mother told her what happened at work, and she wants to check if everything is all right. Obviously, she knows about his hope for a promotion. Everyone does. He talked about it all the time. But now, just thinking of it makes him bitter.

"Don't worry too much about it. They kept you, so it means they still want you there. And you have your annual evaluation in two months, right? So ask for your promotion then."

As if it's that easy. What does she not understand about the word "frozen"?

Marcus cannot help but answer, *"Well, you are quite an optimist, aren't you? That's not going to fly. I am just being realistic here."*

Marcus's answer is resignation disguised as realism. The self-schema of resignation most often derives from avoidance, procrastination or a combination thereof. These behaviours usually compound to the point where it appears there is no way back. And whatever overthinkers were considering will simply not eventuate.

While no one wants to be considered as a pessimist, neither do they want to be optimistic because that would mean being out of touch with reality. But do we really want to be true realists?

If we know that 9 out of 10 startups fail[7] and go bankrupt within their first three years, why even start one? Similarly, more than 85% of French medical students will not pass their first-year exam[8] and fail to become a doctor. So why choose this career to begin with? Now, does it benefit the budding entrepreneurs and aspiring doctors to expect things to fail because this is the realistic thing to do? When we let this kind of realism take over, we become resigned.

The cure for resignation is realistic optimism. Walt Disney wonderfully explains it, saying, "*I always like to look on the optimistic side of life, but I am realistic enough to know that life is a complex matter.*"

Realistic optimists do not deny the reality of the current situation, even if it is exigent and tricky. They acknowledge it, but they also believe that things will be better in the future. They have the conviction that things will turn out positively and have hope for the future.

One of the best examples of this realistic optimism came from Dr Martin Luther King. In his famous "I have a dream" speech, King acknowledged how difficult the current race situation was in the United States. Even though slavery had been abolished a century ago after the American Civil War, he recognised that African Americans were still "*crippled by the manacles of segregation and the chains of discrimination*". However, he also spoke of his dream, a vision of a future where "*little Black boys and Black girls will be able to join hands with little White boys and White girls as sisters and brothers*".

He acknowledged his current reality yet held on his hope for the future. Being a realistic optimist means to analyse the situation rationally yet have a tendency to expect favourable outcomes.

When you are in a dire situation and feel defeated, you can use a practical tool called the inversion principle. Imagine the problem solved, the goal attained, the objective met, and then work backward from there, telling the story in reverse.

Begin with the end in mind, stating, "*We made it. It's a success! But it was not a walk in the park.*" The second step is to list everything that could have gone terribly wrong and prevented this happy ending. Then, for each item on the list, find at least one thing you did to prevent it from happening or at the very least reduce its impact.

The inversion principle helps us work towards positive outcomes while remaining grounded in reality, anticipating potential pitfalls. It empowers us to be realistic optimists.

◆◆◆◆◆

Silence on the line. Marcus realises that what he said to his sister was quite blunt and apologises. Adele sighs.

"I understand that you are disappointed with this situation at work. Sure, it's far from ideal. But realistically, will this attitude get you anywhere? Will it get you this promotion?"

"You don't understand, do you? There will be no promotion for quite some time."

"Okay, I got that. And what are you going to do about it? I mean, have you even talked with your manager about it?"

Marcus hasn't.

"And if you cannot get the promotion in your company, can you apply for a better position somewhere else?"
"Well, technically, yes ..." he acknowledges. *"But that would be far from easy."*
"Right, Marcus. Have you ever heard of the inversion principle?"

Key Takeaways

- Our narrative is the story we tell ourselves about ourselves. It brings coherence to our thoughts, emotions and actions.
- As we develop our narrative, it creates generalisation about ourselves, called self-schemas.
- Overthinkers create specific self-schemas to cope with their inner critic, exacerbated by their overthinking. They then incorporate these self-schemas into their narrative.
- Eliminating overthinking forces overthinkers to question their self-schema and narrative structure, threatening their identity, hence why they are reluctant to reduce their overthinking.
- Unfortunately, overthinkers deceive themselves. They falsely believe they adopt positive self-schemas when they are instead negative.
- Overthinkers mistake avoidance for attentiveness. It is typical of the Dreamer persona.
- Overthinkers mistake procrastination for patience. It is typical of the Observer persona.
- Overthinkers mistake resignation for realism.
- Avoidance, procrastination and resignation promote a state of inhibition, where no decision is made and no action is taken.

Dispelling the Lies of the Self

How-To

To know if you are attentive or avoiding:
- You can use the three columns (Predictions, Perceptions and Observations) exercise to ensure you are not extrapolating too much out of little supporting evidence.
- You can also ask yourself if you are afraid the situation you face could become conflictual and leads to you being rejected or hurt. These fears trigger overthinking for Dreamers and are usually accurate predictors of avoiding behaviour.

To know if you are patient or procrastinating:
- Remember the difference between procrastination and patience doesn't lie in the outcomes but in the attitude toward the decision to act.
- Patience is not passive. It is an active choice, which sometimes leads to not doing something.
- You can also ask yourself if you are afraid of the unknown. This fear triggers overthinking for Observers and is usually an accurate predictor of procrastinating behaviour.

To know if you are realistic or resigned:
- Ask yourself if you are looking at the future with optimism while still acknowledging the difficulties you might encounter in the present?
- If you feel defeated, use the inversion principle. Imagine a future where you have accomplished your goals, then work backward to the present moment. As you do so, list everything that could prevent you from achieving the expected results and find a way to eliminate them (or at least reduce their impact).

 To go further, visit lisonmage.com website or directly scan the QR code. You will find additional resources, including downloadable documents, exercises and videos, to help you *Act Before You overThink*.

Chapter 6

Navigating the Paths to Progress

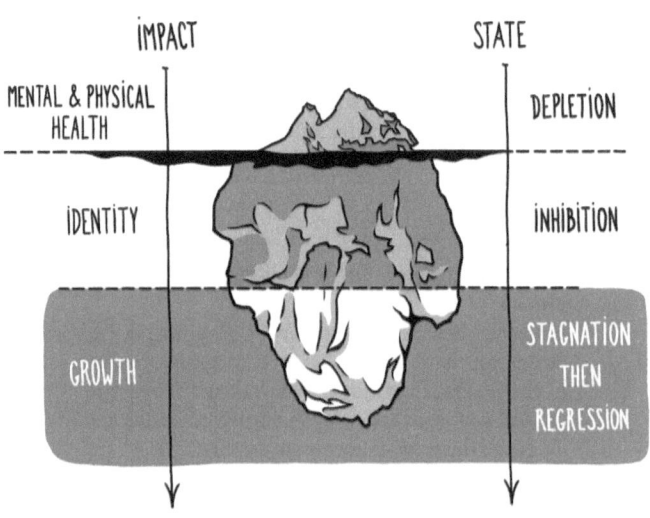

"Life is what you make it. Always has been, always will be."
Eleanor Roosevelt

Navigating the Paths to Progress

Ella and Johann met in their late twenties and have been happily married for more than a decade. They both pursued their corporate careers and progressed steadily. As a result, they have become accustomed to the busy pace of life that goes along with their respective positions.

Viewed from the outside, everything looks perfect. But there is one big cloud that has been hanging over their heads for quite some time now. They are considering having a child and are consumed by questions. Can they handle this responsibility? Will it make them stronger or weaker as a couple? What does it mean for their careers and free time? But the big one that keeps popping up is, do they really want a child?

Every quarter, they organise a special dinner to consider these questions. They prepare a fancy meal, open a bottle of wine and turn off their mobile phones. This is time that is just for them, where they shut out the rest of the world so they can reflect. Then, if they haven't found satisfying answers by the end of the evening, they mutually agree to shelve the issue and revisit it during the next quarterly dinner. This way, they don't let these questions get in the way of their vibrant lives.

But after tonight's dinner, Ella feels numb. How many dinners have they had like this? Eight? Nine? They still haven't decided whether or not this is something they want.

Once more, their choice is postponed to the next quarter.

Overthinking favours avoidance, procrastination and resignation behaviours, pushing us into a state of inhibition. And when we are inhibited, we are more reluctant to do things. As our risk aversion increases, novelty and discovery hold less appeal. Sameness becomes attractive and equated with comfort and relaxation.

This leads to the most pernicious yet most concealed and nefarious consequence of overthinking. If this is overlooked and invisible to so many, it is because it happens over a long period of time.

Act Before You overThink

Picture a raging fire in a wood stove. It burns intensely, but then the air intake is shut off. Without oxygen to stoke the flames, the fire gradually vanishes. Overthinking is a meticulous assassin that slowly murders our internal fire.

Overthinking kidnaps and kills dreams, only leaving us with regrets.

Author Bronnie Ware, who worked as a palliative carer, wrote about the most common regrets she heard from people on their deathbed[1]. And she listed the five following ones at the top of the list:

- I wish I hadn't worked so hard.
- I wish I'd had the courage to live a life true to myself, not the life others expected of me.
- I wish I'd had the courage to express my feelings.
- I wish I'd stayed in touch with my friends.
- I wish that I had let myself be happier.

As you read this, it might seem like common sense. It is evident you should stay in touch with your friends and let yourself be happy. And yet, if this is so obvious, why do so many express these regrets when nearing death?

To answer this question, we have to look at the commonality of these five regrets. They share one unique trait, making them so intense that they are at the top of everyone's mind during their final moments. These regrets are born from an inability to act. They are born from our own inertia. People either decide not to do something or are unable to decide, leading them to do nothing at all.

These regrets about what we didn't do starkly contrast with the regrets we might have about things we did do. For instance, we may regret being rude to someone. We may regret a business decision. We may regret the consequences of our actions, but even if we can't go back in time to prevent them, we still have the ability to fix them. We can apologise. We can make other decisions that will allow our businesses to recover. We can take action to improve the situation, patch a relationship or salvage a career. And over time, the intensity of our regret can diminish. It is like putting some balm on a wound. It won't make it go away, but it will reduce the pain.

Unfortunately, it's just not possible to alleviate the regrets for something we didn't do. There is no way to undo what we never did. We cannot go back in time to the career-defining basketball game and decide to shoot rather than pass to another player. We cannot go back in time to attend this job interview we skipped because we were sure they wouldn't hire us.

Psychology doctors Thomas Gilovich and Victoria Medvec demonstrated that, over time, the intensity of regrets from actions diminishes. But on the contrary, the intensity of regrets from our inaction increases as time passes[2]. This opposition is partially explained by the fact that regrets from inactions are unfinished stories for which we can never have an ending[3]. Our mind is forever left without a firm answer, making these regrets more agonising.

♦♦♦♦♦

On his social media feed, Gregory just saw that Agata, the woman he had a crush on in his teens, has just been married. She looks radiant in her white dress. And he cannot help but feel a twinge of sadness.

What would have happened if he had mustered the courage to talk to her? Would she have accepted his invitation to go out with him? Would he have suffered a painful heartbreak, or would they have stayed together against all odds? Could it have been him in this wedding picture?

Gregory turns off his phone and puts it back in his pocket, closing his eyes. What's the point in thinking about all this? He will never know what could have been.

♦♦♦♦♦

As we imagine how things could have unfolded if we had acted, we create alternative realities. And the difference between our dreams of who we could have become and who we are now causes a hypothetical sense of loss, which gives birth to our regrets from inaction.

The gap between these realities, the "I could have been" and the "I am", widens with time and age. As a result, the loss appears bigger, and we feel worse, which explains why the intensity of our regrets is heightened.

When overthinking inhibits your willingness to act, it pushes you to remain static. But this inertia comes at a price. Regret of inaction is an emotional debt that, sadly, we can never settle. They are like credit card fees we cannot pay off. If these debts—and the interest that accrues—keep on growing, they overwhelm and completely consume overthinkers.

You have probably heard the famous adage from inventor Alexander Graham Bell, "*When one door closes, another door opens.*" It means that if we miss an opportunity or fail to seize it, it creates space for new ones to arise. The issue is that we rarely know the remaining part of this saying, which is, "*But we often look so long and so regretfully upon the closed door that we do not see the ones which open for us.*" This second part is meant to warn us. If we dwell on what is forever gone, we are blind to other avenues we could explore.

Our regrets make us ruminate, stuck to relive past moments as if we were watching a looping video. And while we are trapped with these thoughts, our attention cannot be channelled into other opportunities. We often cannot properly imagine future events or how our current setbacks could simply be stepping stones for successes to come.

This concept is magnificently illustrated with a well-known Chinese parable. A Taoist farmer had been living in the countryside for many years, cultivating his crops. One day, his only horse ran away. When his neighbours heard the news, they came to visit and offered their sympathy. "*This is such bad luck!*" they said, to which the farmer simply replied, "*Maybe.*"

The following morning, to everyone's surprise, the horse had returned, bringing with him three wild horses. "*How wonderful!*" the neighbours exclaimed, to which the farmer answered laconically, "*Maybe.*"

The next day, the farmer's son tried to ride one of the untamed horses. Regrettably, the animal threw him away, and the boy broke his leg in his fall. "*Terrible misfortune!*" the neighbours said. "*Maybe,*" replied the farmer.

A week later, the emperor declared war on a rival nation. Military officers flooded the village, drafting all the eligible young men. Noticing the broken leg of the farmer's son, they passed him over. "*Well, what a good fortune!*" said the neighbours, to which the farmer replied once more, "*Maybe.*"

One of the lessons is that "bad" things come with a silver lining, which will only appear to us in hindsight. Of course, integrating this morale of the story will not immediately dissipate our regrets, but it might appease them. In the end, when we look back at our choices, we can decide how we want to look at them. We determine whether our choices were foolish or clever, whether they diminished us or made us grow.

Although it might not be apparent in the moment "why" something is happening, we have to trust ourselves to take action, even if that means building a new door if none of the existing doors open.

What if you really want to attend a prestigious university but fail the entrance exam? You might regret not studying enough or somehow preparing better. There is no way to know what would have happened if you had, and the "what if" could haunt you until the very end.

But if you take a step back, you can find a way to dissipate this regret. It requires bypassing the dichotomy of your thinking, like believing that there is only one way to enter this university—the entrance exam—with a binary pass or fail result.

What if there is another application process? Could you be sponsored through an apprenticeship? Or gain acceptance due to your sports results? Could you apply to another university that has a partnership with the one you aim to get into, and that would let you go on campus to sit in on some of the courses? And now, what if, through your apprenticeship, your tuition fees are paid for, and you are guaranteed a job when graduating? What if you meet the love of your life at another university? Would you still regret failing the entrance test?

We can only connect the dots looking backward, not forward.

In his commencement speech at Stanford University, Steve Jobs explained that he faced scary prospects and many hardships when he dropped out of college[4]. He had no dorm room, so he had to sleep on his friend's floor. He was returning Coke bottles for the five-cent deposit to pay for his meals. Jobs had closed one door, which led him to open others. After dropping out of college, he attended calligraphy classes. Ten years later, he used this specific knowledge when developing fonts for Apple, which was one of the reasons for Macintosh's success.

We can overcome our regrets as long as we keep opening doors and taking action. But when we fall into the trap of overthinking and enter a state of inhibition, it leads to stagnation down the line, which we mistake for stability.

Stability is relative. It is not constant, no matter how much we might rely on it or plan our lives around it. No sooner do we feel stable than life comes crashing down on us, like a bowling ball hitting pins. Life as we know it can be turned upside down in an instant due to the need to move, relationships beginning or ending, getting or losing a job. Situations that were once stable are no longer so.

The truth is stability is only momentary. But in this brief window of time, we feel relieved and safe. We know where we are and can master our environment. It is comfortable. So, we want to prolong this state. We want to make it last, if possible, forever. Even if permanent stability doesn't exist, we crave it so much that we let ourselves become fooled by it. We settle for what it closely resembles: stagnation.

Stagnation is like working for 10 years in the same company, with no promotion, no new responsibilities, no new colleagues, no new projects. At first, it looks like stability, but we quickly realise this is not comfortable anymore.

Stagnation makes you numb. In stagnation, there is only idleness. Things are frozen. There is no change, progress or growth. And the worst thing is if we stay in stagnation for too long, we will end up in regression.

Like a cliff exposed to the constant impact of the waves, the stillness of stagnation slowly breaks us down. As time passes, the cliff erodes, its structure weakens, and one day it crumbles. Even if you hit pause, life doesn't.

When we bench ourselves and look on from the sideline, we cannot help but notice others' accomplishments, reflecting what we could have done and who we could have been. However, the gap between our current and preferred realities widens as time passes. We realise that our situation did not stagnate, it degraded.

And when we are trapped in stagnation, the only escape is to break out of our comfort zone.

The "comfort zone" concept can be traced back to the work of child development psychologist Lev Vygotsky. He developed the notion of

Act Before You overThink

a zone of proximal development, whereby we only learn a new skill when supported by someone with more knowledge or expertise[5]. It goes beyond what we could learn and do on our own. Someone shows us how to do something, then as we integrate this new skill, we leave the zone of proximal development and can do it without help.

It is like when we learn to play the piano. If we see the sheet music for the first time, we won't be able to read it. We need the help and support from a teacher to learn the basics and then be able to train on our own. And after a few lessons, we master the refrain of one of the most famous compositions of Ludwig van Beethoven, Für Elise. It is now part of our comfort zone.

In our comfort zone, we know things; we are in control. And when we step out of this zone, we enter into our growth zone.

We can explain it as an extension of the zone of proximal development concept. In the growth zone, we are confronted with the unknown. This is risky; we miss pointers or cues and lack knowledge. As a result, we could fail in our undertakings, miss our objectives and fall short of our expectations. Yet, this is where we learn and acquire new skills (with or without external help).

Stepping into our growth zone is like switching from Beethoven's Für Elise to Chopin's Waltz in A minor. Our first attempts will be clunky. We won't be as fluid as when we play Für Elise, but slowly we will get better at it through practice.

When we stay in our growth zone for long enough, we are, in fact, expanding our comfort zone. What was once new and complex becomes familiar and easy. Entering our growth zone is choosing progression over stagnation.

According to Dr Carol Dweck, this choice highlights the differences between two mindsets—the fixed and growth mindsets. Her early studies noticed that children had different reactions when confronted with tricky puzzles[6]. Some reacted with enthusiasm to the challenge, believing it was exciting, whereas others responded negatively, devaluating themselves when failing to perform the task. When given the choice to continue with the complex puzzle or swap for an easier one, the first group of children decided to persevere, whereas the second group gave up.

Building on her findings, Dweck theorised that individuals evolve on a spectrum according to their beliefs about their abilities[7]. On the one hand, people believe their attributes, such as intelligence and talent, are fixed quantities and cannot change (or only under extreme conditions). On the other hand, people believe their attributes can change and grow with practice and effort.

Hence, individuals with a deeply ingrained fixed mindset will perceive failure as a threat. Failing a test demonstrates that they are not good, and since their attributes are inalterable, there is no way to change their conditions, which is a disheartening conclusion to arrive at. Consequently, they avoid trying something new and getting exposed to the risk of failure. They are more inclined to remain in a state of sameness, a state of stagnation. On the contrary, with a growth mindset approach, failure can be perceived as an evaluation, pointing to an area where progress could be made.

And choosing progression over stagnation doesn't require us to do things in great strides. As a matter of fact, it is way easier to take consistent small steps. Each of them becomes a stepping stone, building our momentum to allow us to break free from our inertia, leave our comfort zone and enter our growth zone.

During the 2014 commencement speech of the University of Texas, Admiral McRaven shared his life lessons learned from his time serving as a Navy Seal. He stated that to change the world, we must start by making our bed every morning[8]. As much as it might sound ludicrous, what he meant was that even if everything goes wrong with our day, we still did one thing right. We get home after an exhausting day, lie down in bed, and are able to say to ourselves, "*At least the bed is well made. The room doesn't look like a mess.*"

Small wins can help us redirect our attention from the negative to the positive, quieting our inner critic and fear of failure. They help us to overcome our internal resistance. They create an impulse, mentally and physically, that gets us going. They generate momentum.

When we complete a task, even a tiny one, we get a feel-good sensation as our body releases dopamine. It creates pleasure, like when you eat chocolate. And our brain remembers it and will seek more of it[9].

When you feel defeated and an insidious voice inside you is saying, "*It's okay, it can wait until later. I'll do it tomorrow,*" ask yourself, what is your small win today? Is it making your bed? Going for a morning walk or run? Practising Spanish for 15 minutes? Getting the kids to school on time? Your small wins energise you. They empower you. They build a dynamic to allow you to leave your comfort zone and effortlessly enter your growth zone.

And when we enter our growth zone and hit a snag, we need to show ourselves compassion. We cannot constantly be challenged or tested. It's normal to go back in our comfort zone from time to time, to regroup, recover and rise again.

Self-compassion is defined as the ability to treat oneself with warmth and understanding in difficult times and recognising that making mistakes is part of being human. It can help us diminish the effects of overthinking and protect us from harsh self-judgement[10]. Dr Kristen Neff, an expert in self-compassion, worked to establish fundamental clarifications on this concept[11].

Firstly, self-compassion is not self-pity. Instead of feeling sorry for ourselves and isolating ourselves, we step back, look objectively at the situation and recognise that our difficulties are temporary, and many people have been through the same thing.

Secondly, self-compassion is not self-indulgence. It is not a free pass to do whatever we want, whenever we want. It is the ability to see the entirety of the situation, with its drawbacks and intricacies, and yet show ourselves kindness.

Self-compassion doesn't judge, it empathises and supports. But more broadly, it encompasses the notions of mindfulness, kindness and perhaps, the most important, to recognise our common humanity.

This last element refers to the ability to appreciate that as a consequence of being human, we are imperfect—we have flaws and sometimes fail. And while being aware that anyone can encounter difficulties doesn't make our situation any easier, it relieves us of our feeling of inadequacy and can even enhance our motivation.

To practise self-compassion, you can use this effective and pragmatic exercise. Imagine what you would say to a close friend or family member facing the exact same situation you are in.

It could be that you just received an email stating that your application for your dream company has been rejected. You went to the interview, knowing it would be difficult. You didn't have the best qualifications. You didn't have the most experience. You answered wrongly to a few technical questions. You went out of your comfort zone, and it didn't work out. It would be easy to start criticising yourself.

As you notice this, adopt a third-person point of view. Imagine yourself as a compassionate observer. What would you tell yourself then?

You can start with mindful empathy. "*I know this is disappointing, and this is not the result you were expecting.*" Next, you could bring attention to your common humanity, saying, "*It happens to everyone, even the best.*" Kindly add, "*This failure doesn't define you. You are so much more.*" And conclude by broadening the horizon: "*And maybe they have other positions you could apply to.*"

◆◆◆◆◆

Johann picks up on Ella's worries and decides to bring forward their quarterly dinner.

But this time, he has also invited an acquaintance, Tracey, a midwife at their local hospital, three blocks away. The ambience is a bit awkward at first, especially when Johann explains that they kept postponing their decision even though they had been thinking about having a baby for more than two years. But Tracey simply nods, encouraging them to keep going.

Then, as Ella and Johann finish telling their story, there is a brief moment of silence. Tracey looks at both of them with a warm smile.

"This is an important decision. It could completely change your life, so it is normal to think about it and have all these questions. I have seen many couples go through this, and it can take time."

As she says this last sentence, an invisible weight seems to fall off the couple's shoulders.

"I believe it is quite brave to have this conversation between the two of you. Some people don't even talk about it."

She pauses before continuing.

"Now, you can't just keep thinking about it because if you don't choose, you will eventually run out of time and the choice will be made for you. And ultimately, you could end up regretting it."

Another pause.

"I understand it is hard, but maybe you could look at it a bit differently. For example, have you considered adopting instead of having your own baby? Some couples I know who decide not to have children volunteer for organisations that help young kids."

They look at her, a bit startled. They had never thought about these possibilities.

"Indeed, this is different, but since you seem stuck in your decision, this might broaden your options."

Key Takeaways

- When we overthink, we enter a state of inhibition, where we prefer sameness over novelty.
- This inaction can create life-long regrets, which we can never completely get rid of.
- Contrary to regrets about things we did, the intensity of regrets from things we didn't do increases over time.
- To avoid regrets, inhibited overthinkers chase a mirage—permanent stability—and end up settling in stagnation.
- Unfortunately, staying for too long in stagnation leads to regression.
- Even if we hit pause, life doesn't. If we remain static, the gap between our current and preferred realities widens and we will, sooner or later, realise the situation didn't stagnate, it degraded.
- We can choose progression over stagnation. It requires moving forward and challenging ourselves, leaving our comfort zone to enter our growth zone.
- Staying in our growth zone will, in fact, expand our comfort zone. Things that were once new and complex become familiar and easy.
- To progress, we don't need to do things in great strides. Instead, we can take consistent small steps and leverage the momentum they create.
- At times, it is normal to go back to our comfort zone to recover and replenish before challenging ourselves again.

How-To

When we look back at our choices regretfully, we can do the following:
- Remember that when one door closes, others open.
- Even if it is often difficult to realise it in the moment, you need to move forward and take action.
- If you cannot see any door, you might have to create it. It usually requires taking a step back to escape a binary approach, like only being able to attend university if we pass its entrance exam.
- As you do so, imagine if there are any other solutions to achieve your goal, like being sponsored through an apprenticeship.

As you keep on opening doors, taking action, you will progress and avoid stagnation. To create and maintain this momentum:
- Remember you need to challenge yourself regularly, not constantly. It is normal to rest and recover in your comfort zone to then be able to do something new in your growth zone.
- Focus on small achievements to motivate yourself
- Use self-compassion when encountering a setback.

To practice self-compassion:
- Remember it is not self-pity or self-indulgence, but the ability to treat yourself with warmth and understanding when facing difficulties, while recognising that making mistakes is part of being human.
- Talk to yourself as you would do with a dear friend going through a tough time.

To go further, visit lisonmage.com website or directly scan the QR code. You will find additional resources, including downloadable documents, exercises and videos, to help you *Act Before You overThink*.

Conclusion of the Second Myth

In this section, we unveiled and pinpointed the harmful nature of overthinking.

We put it on stage and turned on all the lights. Then, with nowhere to hide, we stripped it of its disguise and exposed it for what it truly is.

Overthinking is an illness, a liar and an assassin.

Overthinking is an illness that can cause negative affects such as anxiety, stress and worry. It will also sustain, amplify and perpetuate these emotional states and can lead to damaging psychological pathologies like clinical anxiety, chronic stress and depression.

And more often than not, mental disorders will spill over into our physical health. Overthinking can impact the quality and duration of our sleep and also relates to eating disorders. Overthinking depletes us. It drains us of our energy.

Overthinking is also a liar. It deceives us while claiming to act in our best interest. It sabotages our sense of self and lures us towards inhibitive behaviours that keep us in a state where nothing happens.

Overthinking is like a master trickster, fooling us into believing that avoidance, procrastination and resignation is attentiveness, patience and realism. And when we try to catch it red-handed, this toxic partner has the nerve to answer us, *"Look what I am doing for you! Don't you see it is for your own good? How can you be so ungrateful?"*

But when left unchecked for too long, overthinking reveals its most revolting aspect.

Overthinking is an assassin. It is different from a murderer, who often impulsively acts when enraged or terrified. Instead, overthinking is calculating, methodical and relentless. It scrupulously plans its hits, with one specific and unique target: our growth.

Given time, overthinking kills dreams, aspirations and hopes. It poisons the soil of our being, making sure nothing can sprout and blossom. And when it has accomplished its mission, all we are left with are life-long regrets.

Now, let me ask you this question: would you hang out with someone who literally makes you sick, constantly lies to you and plans on bludgeoning your unique potential?

The answer is, obviously, no.

Overthinking is not "fine" and will never be. We should not stick with it. We should cut the cord and part ways as soon as possible. Overthinking is a severe problem, with terrible consequences, and coming to this realisation dissipates our second myth.

Third Myth

Overthinking is Inevitable in Decision-Making

We have made significant progress by dispelling the two first myths of overthinking: recognising it doesn't make us think better and seriously impacts us.

Yet we can still feel profoundly vulnerable.

As we come to terms with the reality of overthinking and the absolute necessity to overcome it, it also appears that overthinking is working in insidious ways. It is always there, lurking, deeply rooted inside us. It is as if we have no control over it.

No matter how aware we are, we catch ourselves overthinking again and again. It can feel like throwing ourselves in the middle of an unwinnable battle or fighting against a strong river current, irresistibly pushing us towards a dangerous waterfall.

Overthinking feels inevitable, like a curse imposed on us. We are prisoners of our minds, jailed in an inescapable labyrinth. Entangled in our thoughts, we resign ourselves to our tragic fate.

But there is a way out.

Overthinking is Inevitable in Decision-Making

In Greek mythology, King Theseus was tasked to kill the Minotaur, a half-human, half-beast creature that was haunting an inextricable maze. To ensure he could escape safely, his lover Ariadne gave him a ball of red thread. Attaching one end at the entrance of the monster's hideout, he unrolled it on his way in and, like breadcrumbs, rolled it back to find his way out. So, like Theseus, we can defeat our Minotaur and escape the overthinking labyrinth, using an Ariadne's string.

In this last section, we will burst the third myth of overthinking. We will dissipate madness with a practical method. We will make our own Ariadne's string.

To do so, we need to understand that overthinking is not something we are destined to live with forever but a bad habit we fall into almost unconsciously. As a consequence, overthinking is a self-taught mental pattern we can unlearn.

Like any other habit, it is composed of three elements: the trigger, the behaviour and the reward[1].

The trigger is the event that creates the impulse to perform the behaviour. Then the behaviour will be rewarding somehow, often through dopamine release at the biological level.

For instance, a trigger could be that we receive an email from an unsatisfied customer, making us stressed. In reaction, we impulsively go to the fridge to pick up some chocolate, a comforting behaviour. Eating the chocolate feels good in the moment, giving us a small reward.

The "feel good" sensation teaches us to repeat the behaviour because we want to be rewarded again. It creates a reinforcing loop and strengthens our habits. After a few repetitions, every time we feel stressed, we compulsively want to eat some sweets, and we struggle to explain this craving or make it go away.

Overthinking is the behaviour of a maladaptive habit, similar to a sugar craving. And like any habit, we can learn to break it.

Act Before You overThink

The first thing to do is to stop the pattern by removing the rewards. We already worked on this in the two first sections. With the first myth, overthinking made us feel good because we associated it with improved thinking. With the second myth, overthinking made us feel good because we associated it with the positive traits: attentiveness, patience and realism. As we invalidate these beliefs, the act of overthinking doesn't pay off anymore. It is like eating chocolate that tastes like Brussels sprouts (or something you despise). We negate the rewarding part of our mental habit to help us stop this behaviour.

Unfortunately, removing the rewards might not be enough to change our habits. Researchers trained participants to respond to a visual test on a computer screen, rewarding them with sweets. Measuring their brain activity, they found out that even if there is no reward anymore, a visual cue on the computer could still drive participants to action[2]. Simply put, scientists found that a habit might persist even when the reward is not part of the pattern loop anymore.

In our case, it means that some situations will still lead us to overthink, even if we know this is detrimental to us. Like a weird remark our manager makes or when faced with a difficult decision. But these are triggers we can identify. We can recognise that these events are likely to make us overthink, and then we can use a technique called habit stacking, which requires us to pair another behaviour with our triggers. And this is our Ariadne's string! This is the way out of the maze of our thoughts.

When we notice the triggering situation, especially for decision-making, we need to fall back on simple mental models to dissipate our overthinking behaviour. These mental models assist us in understanding the triggering situation better and support us in our decision-making process.

Mental models are just lenses through which we can see and analyse the world. They perform the role of a filter when making decisions. Specifically, they hide some information and highlight others.

Most importantly, they should be easy to apply. Mental models should be practical, quick and easy to use. The best ones can often be summed up in one question.

So, to fight the last myth, we use a combination of three of the most useful mental models to form a decision-making prism I called the freedom filters.

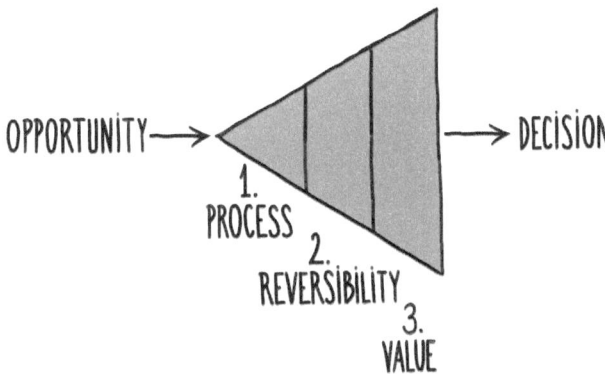

As we explained, we use the freedom filters when a situation activates our overthinking. In this model, the trigger has been renamed opportunity. By doing so, we remind ourselves that a triggering situation might have downsides but could also offer upsides. This slight yet meaningful change unconsciously allows us to be more broadminded in our approach.

Then, we analyse the opportunity through the first filter, decorrelating our thought process from the immediate outcome, enabling us to maximise our chances of success over time.

With the second filter, we advantageously trade the decision's reversibility to increase our confidence and satisfaction in our choice.

With the last filter, we learn to make hard decisions effortlessly.

Equipped with our Ariadne's string, the freedom filters, fighting our overthinking is not an unwinnable battle anymore. As we learn to use this tool, we can stop being stuck in ruminating thoughts, especially when we have to make decisions like choosing a university or buying a flat.

Chapter 7

Trusting the Process

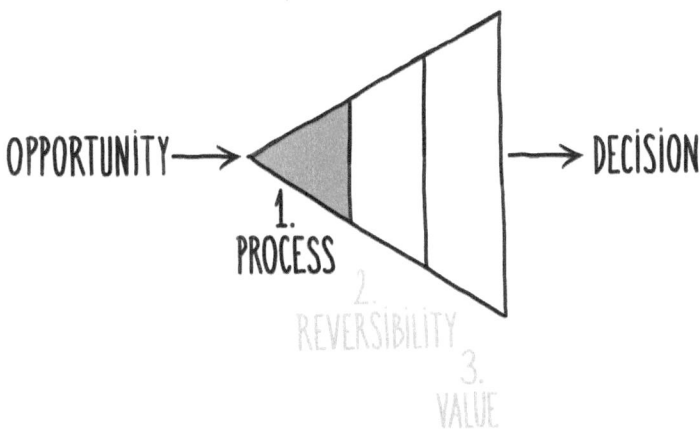

"If you can't describe what you are doing as a process, you don't know what you're doing."

W. Edwards Deming

Arturo is looking for a present for his friend, Matias. But like always, he finds this tedious. Even if they know each other quite well, he struggles to find a good gift idea.

And there is some anxiety building up as the birthday approaches. The last thing Arturo wants is for Matias to pretend he likes it and then hide his present in his basement or throw it away.

Plus, there will be so many people he knows at this party; what if he picks the wrong gift and people judge him for it? How much should he spend? If he buys something cheap, what would people think? But if it is too expensive, it would make Matias embarrassed.

Arturo is undecided because his friend already has "everything" he needs. He probably should not buy something decorative as there is too much risk it won't match his style. Matias is not big on reading, so a book is out of the question. Since everybody will buy a bottle of wine, maybe he should too? But Matias might still be disappointed. He got him a bottle for his last birthday and it's still in his liquor cabinet.

On Matias's birthday, Arturo still doesn't have a gift. He has been thinking about it for more than a month, yet he still hasn't decided. He has a list with a dozen ideas, but he struggles to choose, always finding a reason why they are the wrong choice.

As he is short on time, he needs to pick something. He can't come empty-handed, so he goes with his safest option: a gift card. It is bland and unexciting, but at least Matias will be able to choose something he likes.

When we have to make a decision, we apply our thinking to analyse our options to get a good outcome. But we also want to get to this result the right way.

For Arturo, a good result means picking the right gift for his friend. He is mentally going through a process to make his decision, asking himself questions like what does my friend like? Or what is appropriate for a birthday? And in an ideal world, a suitable process leads to a good outcome.

On the other hand, an inefficient process should result in poor outcomes. Arturo would not randomly decide what he should buy. If he does, he will most certainly end up offering a present that Matias doesn't like.

But what happens at the intersection of these two scenarios? Would you rather have a suitable process but a poor outcome or a flawed process with a good outcome?

Imagine the following situation. As a manager reviewing a job application, you gather the input from all the team members about the kind of person with whom they want to work and see if the applicant matches the criteria. Then, you talk to HR about the applicant's interview, who gives you positive feedback. Finally, you do your due diligence, calling and checking her three references. Solely after validating all these steps, you decide to hire this person. Unfortunately, she resigns after two weeks into the job.

In another situation, you decide to hire, on the spot, a person after a 10-minute chat at a networking event based on a gut feeling. Later, you find out she is a genius, does incredible work and is a pleasure to work with.

In the first case, you worked a lot and have nothing to show for it. In the second, you did the bare minimum and got great results. So, when asked which of these situations is better, it's a no-brainer for many of us. It is like asking Arturo if he prefers meticulously choosing a gift and seeing his friend disappointed or picking the first item he finds in the gift shop but delighting Matias.

The reason why we favour the second solution is we are biased towards outcomes rather than processes. Namely, we prefer a good outcome over a suitable process.

Act Before You overThink

Several studies exposed this outcome bias. One of the most dramatic ones presented the following scenario for participants to evaluate the quality of the decision.

In their fabricated story, a 55-year-old man has a heart condition, forcing him to stop working because of chest pain. A specific bypass operation would relieve his pain and increase his life expectancy by five years. However, 8% of the people die as a result of this operation. Nevertheless, the surgeon recommends going ahead with the procedure at the hospital.

The researchers then created two endings for their story. In one, participants are told the man survives the operation. In the other, they are told he died from complications.

Both groups have to rate the quality of the surgeon's decision with the information he has before the operation, meaning the doctor doesn't know the outcome. Surprisingly, the first group rated the quality of the decision from the surgeon better than the second group[1]. Both groups should have rated the decision roughly the same if they had followed a purely rational approach, but they didn't because they had one piece of information the surgeon didn't have: the outcome. The first group rated the decision higher because the outcome was positive. It shows that unconsciously the outcome holds greater weight than the process when we evaluate a decision.

We can partially explain this behaviour with the fact we link the outcome with performance. This association is instilled in our thinking from a young age. It starts at school with the grading system. We look at how well we performed more than how hard we studied, so the learning process ends up mattering less than the outcome.

If we study diligently, it usually enables us to get good marks. But sometimes it is not enough. Our efforts and learning process are not always rewarded. And if we want to get into a specific university, our application is not judged based on our learning process but our grades. Hence, it doesn't matter if we are lucky, cheat or study hard to get in since, in the end, we only value the outcome.

Likewise, at work, we are also rewarded for our performance. For instance, if we work as a sales representative, we are incentivised on the quarterly turnover associated with our signed contracts. If we are a project manager, our evaluation is tied to achieving the project's milestones on time and on budget.

If we don't look at how this is achieved, it can be tempting to sell a product that our customer doesn't need, or cut corners in software testing exposing to potential defects to ensure we meet our performance targets. We would adopt an unhealthy process to get "excellent" results.

We are conditioned to focus on the outcome of our decisions rather than the decision-making process.

Consequently, when we face decisions, we often examine them solely through the lens of their expected outcomes. It doesn't matter whether or not making this decision is correctly articulated or comes from an adequate reflection—we are only focusing on the results.

MALADAPTIVE DECISION EVALUATION MATRIX

	OUTCOME	
PROCESS	POOR OR FAILED ATTEMPT	EXCELLENT OR SUCCESSFUL ATTEMPT
INADEQUATE OR DEFICIENT	☹	☺
SUITABLE	☹	☺

We can then quickly schematise our decision process with a two-by-two matrix. We are happy when we have a good result and unhappy when we don't. In this case, we completely ignore how we got the results. This excessive focus on the outcome instead of the process is a maladaptive habit that invariably leads to poor decisions.

The reason is that unless you are dealing with particular cases, life is difficult to predict. Therefore, there is always some uncertainty about the outcome.

How about a promised promotion that is supposedly 100% secured but now off the table due to poor company results? Was it a "bad" decision to work intensively and ask for a raise? Or what about a holiday you have been waiting impatiently for weeks that now has to be cancelled because you fell down the stairs and broke your legs? Was it a "bad" decision to plan this getaway?

In hindsight, it is easy to blame ourselves for our lack of foresight.

Our inner critic is screaming at us that we should have known better. And we are vulnerable to overthinking when our decisions produce poor outcomes or failed attempts. We can fall back into patterns described in the previous sections, such as trying to make the uncertainty disappear with an excess of analytical thinking or overanalysing what we could have done differently to get better results.

So, to liberate ourselves from overthinking, we need to use our first freedom filter: the process filter.

The aim is to shift our focus from outcome to process. It starts by replacing the question we ask ourselves when making a decision. The question changes from, "*Will I be successful?*" to "*What are the steps to succeed consistently?*" The difference highlights three key points.

1. Process always comes before outcome.
2. Process influences outcome.
3. Process and outcome tie with a temporal notion of regularity.

The two first points emphasise the importance of thinking in process rather than outcome. Actually, this is a profound mindset shift, which allows us to update how we evaluate our decisions. It stresses the quality of the decision-making process independently of the decision outcomes.

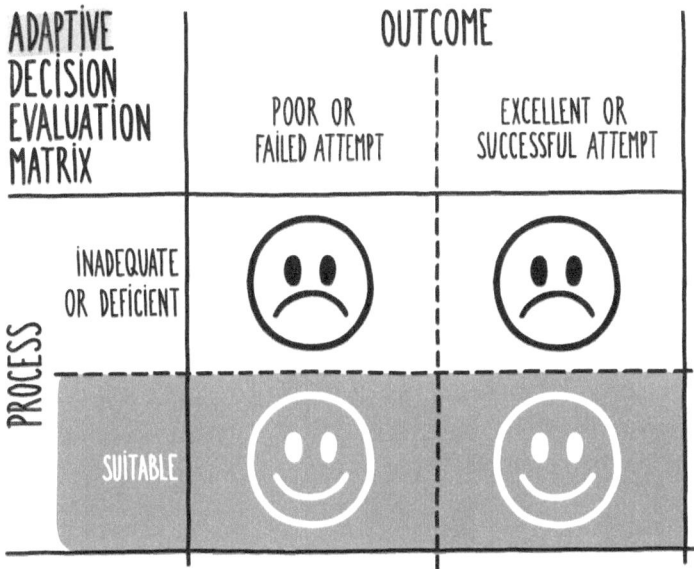

We can update our decision matrix. We observe that it doesn't matter if we failed or succeeded, we are solely looking at the nature of our process. If it is suitable, we should be happy and proud of ourselves.

Let's take a specific example, like wishing to become wealthy, to illustrate why we should focus on the process more than the outcome. Most of us know that going to the casino and gambling all our savings at the roulette is a poor strategy because the odds are against us.

The casino always has an edge against the players. It is called the "house advantage" and represents the average amount a player will lose relative to any bet made. Indeed, this can be calculated, and even in its fairest version (the European one), the "house advantage" is 2.70%. This means that the player is expected to lose 0.027 dollars for every dollar bet. I am not a financial expert, but it seems pretty evident that losing money for every dollar invested is an inadequate process to becoming wealthy.

The trick is that we could be lucky once and win big. It would be a perfect instance of using a deficient process to obtain a successful outcome. And the payout is impressive. If we bet $10 on a single number, we would end up with $350. Unfortunately, this prospect of winning a big prize triggers a cognitive bias called the possibility effect[2]. The thrill of earning a large amount of money and the appeal of pleasant fantasies push us to disregard the actual probabilities (thus the quality of the process) to only focus on the possibility of a good outcome.

Indeed, the roulette game is a manifest example of a deficient process—gambling—invariably driving us to poor outcomes, only one of which is losing money.

Yet, its point stands. There are many situations in life where we can be blindsided by the possibility of a good outcome and neglect the reliability of the process.

For example, our selling practice might get us wins across the board until customers decide they don't want to work with us again. If an issue occurred in the project, a root-cause analysis might point out our neglect. Thus, one of the benefits of the process filter is to reduce our biases, which are irrationally pushing us to favour outcomes.

And I experienced first-hand why we should focus on the process rather than the outcome when undertaking the project to write this book. Indeed, I wanted to put my best work out, and since this is my first book, I felt overwhelmed with the task.

As a result, I read a lot. I read other self-development books, decision-making books, and books on writing and publishing a book. Then I attended webinars on how to write a book. I watched YouTube videos, talked with publishers, chatted with editors and exchanged with authors. I gathered an immense amount of information, compulsively reading more, consuming more information. However, I hadn't written a single line.

Surely by now, you can see the pattern here. I was literally overthinking it, solely focusing on the outcome, namely, writing a "good book", but I was paralysed every time I faced my computer, looking at a blank page in front of me. My ideas were all over the place. I had so much material from all my interviews I didn't know where to begin. Sometimes there would be days where I would think about the book but not do a single thing to advance it.

So, I needed to find a process to help me (and actually, I ended up with more than one). The first and main one I applied was a concept the author Steven Pressfield explained in his book *The War of Art*.

I was facing what he calls Resistance, an internal force preventing me from doing, from writing. It could take many forms, like procrastination or avoidance. I could not rely on willpower alone to defeat it. I had to have a system to back me up. And it is quite a simple one. I needed to get "in the trenches" every day: sit in front of my computer, and write, come hell or high water.

Quality and quantity were details of the process that I could adjust, but the main point was to write, no matter what. So, I had time blocked in my calendar—at the hour, every day—to write. It became a routine. There was no excuse to avoid it. Every day, I progressed, getting closer to my goal, to my "good" outcome of getting a book written and published.

So, the lesson from Pressfield's wisdom, which applies to everyone, is that amateurs have goals and professionals have systems.

Amateurs focus and dream of the potential outcomes while professionals know and apply processes to achieve the outcomes they aim for.

There is a story that is often used in leadership training when attempting to inspire your team. This is the tale of breaking the four-minute-mile barrier. For nine consecutive years, no runner had been able to run a mile in under four minutes. Several athletes got close, but no one could achieve it. At the time, sports commentators prophesied it could be out of human reach, that our body was not made to run at such a speed.

In 1957, Roger Bannister broke the record with a time of 3:59.4 minutes. Two months following his exploit, two other runners got below four minutes, and since then, the list just kept on growing. Many say the actual barrier to pass below the four-minute threshold was psychological and that Bannister's achievement allowed others to overcome their mental block.

If it is undeniable that the right mindset is needed to overcome one's limitations, the incompleteness of this story is harmful. When people tell this anecdote, they focus on the narrative, "*He didn't know it was impossible, so he did it,*" which is inspiring but unrealistic and seriously lacking in pragmatism. The rest of the story is that serious progress was made in training techniques, nutrition and coaching at that period. The right processes to reach the outcomes were adopted and refined by an expanding number of athletes.

Bannister made history, but he was not the only one with a conquering mindset, aiming for the record. If he hadn't won the record at that specific race, he would have won it at another, or maybe another competitor would have broken the record and stolen the headlines[3]. Sooner or later, the track record would have fallen because professionals focus on the processes to reach the outcome, not the outcome in itself.

Not only does this allow professionals to accomplish what they set themselves out to do, but it also tilts the scale to ensure the playground is even or in their favour. They create their own "house advantage" by lowering luck's role in their successes.

In her book *Thinking in Bets*, behavioural scientist and star poker player Annie Duke talks about how we can eventually remove luck from the equation when we decorrelate the process from the outcome.

Trusting the Process

This is one of the fundamentals she had to learn in order to win her poker championships. To increase your odds of success, you must concentrate on the play, not the result. If you were to consider a seven and a two of different colours to be a "good" hand (it is actually one of the worst hands possible) because you won last time, you are up for a disappointing surprise.

Clearly, there are many other layers of complexity when analysing a play, but what all pro-players do when they review their plays together is to explain what happened, the cards they had, etc., but they omit one thing: the outcome of the play.

Consequently, when they present a play to their peers, they don't reveal the result to avoid being biased in their judgement. It allows them to review whether the thought process was "right", meaning offering the highest chance of success, even if you ended up losing. The reason is that you want to repeat plays with a high probability of winning and discard the ones with lower chances. Play by play, they learn how to refine the decision-making process, which, in the long run, reduces the influence of luck on the outcomes. And they are more likely to win.

More importantly, Duke also shows that thinking in process requires a mindset shift. We need to shy away from binary thinking to embrace probabilistic thinking. A decision is not "right" or "wrong" based on the outcome. Instead, a decision offers a certain probability of achieving a successful outcome.

For instance, when the weather forecast announces an 80% chance of rain for tomorrow and the next day, it is tempting to think the meteorologists were wrong if we don't see a drop of water. But they were not. And strangely enough, they were not right either. Instead, we can say that they are accurate over time.

When they forecast 80%, it means that it will rain eight times out of 10. Therefore, if the weather forecast states that there is an 80% chance of rain for 10 days in a row, it should rain eight days out of 10. If you look only at one day out of the 10, you could end up on one of the two sunny days and wrongly assume *"these guys truly know nothing about the weather"*. In reality, weather forecasts are highly accurate if you assess them over a long period.

Like poker, weather forecasts are judged over time. Incongruities are smoothed out. If we are unlucky once and get a poor outcome, it doesn't mean we have a "wrong" process. It might simply mean we are getting the two days of sun out of our 10-day period. As a consequence, the outcomes of our processes must be evaluated over time.

So, when we face a decision where we could start overthinking, using our process filter, we can ask ourselves, "*Am I focusing on the outcome or on the process?*" And it is sometimes difficult to make the distinction. A substitution, although imperfect, can be, "*Am I focusing on what I cannot control or what I can?*"

In the end, there is no way to know with total certainty if the candidate we are hiring will end up being a brilliant recruit. But we can ensure if her mentality and values fit with the company and the team with an interview. We can check if she has successfully completed similar projects by calling references. We can evaluate her ability to handle challenging and novel tasks with a test.

Alas, when we transition and start our new processes, it can be scary because we are unsure what to do precisely. We will quickly notice our failed attempts, which can make us doubt the process. We question ourselves, wondering if we should stick with this novel method.

If we are tempted to fall back into overthinking, submerged in counterfactual thinking, we should remind ourselves of the adage, "One swallow does not a summer make" from Aesop's fable, *The Young Man and the Swallow*.

In this tale, a young man loses all his money due to poor choices. All he has left is a coat to keep him warm. As he sees a swallow passing by, he interprets it as a sign that spring is coming and decides to sell his coat to make a bet, hoping to make up for his previous decisions. Not only does he lose his coat and money once more, but he also notices the weather is not improving. Shortly after, he finds the swallow frozen to death, realising he was deceived.

Among the many lessons this fable conveys, the one we should remember here is that one instance of an event cannot accurately predict a trend. We should see several swallows before conclusively deducing that the migration cycle has started and winter is ending.

It is like going to the gym. If we look at our weight loss after exercising for a week, we will probably not observe impressive results. In fact, we might even have gained weight in the beginning. To see if our training plan is a suitable process, we should regularly monitor our weight to get enough data points to establish a representative trend.

We cannot analyse our evolution with only one measurement after our first week of training. With two points, we get an idea, but if one is wrong, our interpretation can be completely erroneous.

What if we step on the scale in the wrong spot and it misreads our weight? Or what if the ground the scale is on is not level? Alternatively, after two months of training (and sweating) and eight weekly measurements, we will start to have enough results to get a valid interpretation.

So, to evaluate our process, we need to go through it often, even if our first attempts are not successful.

And to overcome this initial barrier, our resistance and the overthinking that might ensue, we can use the power of "yet".

It is a simple word, yet it is so powerful. You might notice the difference between these two sentences: "*I cannot do this*" and "*I cannot do this yet*". It changes our perspective, the timeline and the result. Most importantly, it underlines the journey.

We need to look at our progression, not our destination.

If our evolution is positive, if we observe some regular progress, then we know our process is suitable. It puts us on the right path. We know that as long as we keep on, we will end up reaching our destination. When we progress over time, we gain certainty to achieve our expected outcomes.

And there is another advantage to following a process that makes us grow. When we look at our journey, what we have accomplished over the last three months, the last year, the last decade, we are able to acknowledge our progress and be proud of ourselves.

Progress makes the process enjoyable, motivated and satisfying.

As Arturo drives to Matias's place to celebrate his birthday with the other guests, he can't stop thinking about the possible reactions his friend will have when he unwraps his present.

He starts criticising and mocking his choice. "*Seriously?! A gift card? You couldn't have got something more personalised?*" He sighs, slowly shaking his head and wondering if he is really a good friend.

When he arrives, Arturo takes the gift to the door and forces himself to smile. The last thing he wants is to look depressed as Matias welcomes him. He rings at the entrance, the door opens and he is greeted warmly.

"*Arturo! I'm so happy you came!*"

Suddenly, he doesn't need to force his smile. Matias's happiness is contagious. However, he is still nervous while giving his gift.

"*Here. A little bird told me today is special.*"

Matias replies, "*It seems you're well informed!*"

He takes the present and begins to open it.

Trusting the Process

Arturo suddenly feels his anxiety rising as he carefully watches Matias's reaction.

"*Oh! A gift card! Thanks!*"

Matias keeps on smiling. Is he genuinely happy with the gift card? He did not spot a mimic hinting otherwise.

"*You know, that's great; I needed new earphones, so I'll probably use the card to get a new pair.*"

Arturo is relieved, but his friend continues.

"*You know, I'm thrilled you're here. And offering me a gift, this is awesome. I love the intention. It means a lot to me.*"

With the party going on and his stress decreasing, Arturo thinks again about Matias's reaction. Maybe any gift would have pleased him? Could he care more about the intent? Was it all in the process of offering something?

Key Takeaways

- We are conditioned to focus on the outcome of our decisions rather than the decision-making process.
- Hence, we would rather follow a flawed process if we get a good outcome than a suitable process leading to a poor outcome.
- To liberate ourselves from overthinking, we have to focus more on decision-making processes (systems) than outcomes (goals).
- Amateurs have goals, dreaming of the potential outcomes, while professionals have systems. They know and apply processes to achieve the outcomes they aim for.
- Embracing processes requires a shift from binary thinking—is it right or wrong based on the outcome achieved?—to probabilistic thinking—what are the chances to achieve the outcome with this process?
- This new thinking helps us understand that a poor outcome doesn't necessarily mean we follow an inefficient process.
- To make a valid assessment of the reliability and regularity of a process, we must evaluate it over time with a large enough sample of outcomes.
- The process filter can be summarised by the question "Am I focusing on the outcome or the process?"
- If it is difficult to make the distinction, you can substitute the question with "Am I focusing on what I cannot control or what I can?"

How-To

When we start using new processes, it can be difficult to overcome our resistance and even persevere when we have poor outcomes. To help us go through this initial phase, we can use the power of "yet":

- We are simply adding "yet" in our daily vocabulary. Instead of "I cannot do it", "I don't understand it" and "I haven't done it", we say "I cannot do it yet", "I don't understand it yet" and "I haven't done it yet".
- It helps us recognise we are a "work in progress".
- It emphasises the journey. We don't try to "be good", we want to "get better".
- We are almost unconsciously reframing the situation to remain engaged and motivated.

Additionally, to focus on processes rather than outcomes, we look at evolution trends to check whether we are on the right path or not. If we are, it means we are progressing, and it reinforces our conviction that, sooner or later, we will reach our destination.

It is also essential to remain concentrated on our progression. If we do observe the ones from others, it should only be to learn from them how we can improve our own processes, not to compare outcomes.

To go further, visit lisonmage.com website or directly scan the QR code. You will find additional resources, including downloadable documents, exercises and videos, to help you *Act Before You overThink*.

Chapter 8

Trading up Decisions Reversibility

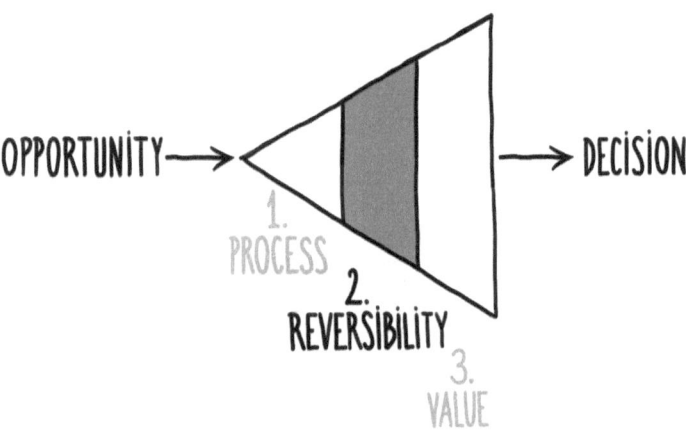

"You can't go back and change the beginning, but you can start where you are and change the ending."

C.S Lewis

Zoe has just finished high school and is considering which university to apply to. She diligently categorises the information that seems relevant to make her decision. She catalogues the courses' curricula, checks the teachers' credentials and employment rates for various jobs after graduation. She also looks at the tuition fees and their different financing options.

Once her research is completed, she shortlists three suitable universities. Then, she visits each university, looks at the campus's infrastructures, and discusses with students and teachers.

As she finishes her last university inspection, Zoe is completely lost in her thoughts while driving home. She feels overwhelmed and more undecided than ever. All three options appear fantastic on paper and are even better in reality.

How is she going to choose between them?

That's such a big commitment in time and money; she cannot afford a mistake. This decision will influence her life forever. Zoe followed her plan to the letter and thought that doing her deep investigation would help her make up her mind, but right now, she has no idea which university to pick and truly feels helpless.

If having a good process undeniably gives us an edge, it might not be enough to stop overthinking our decisions. In this case, we first need to get back to the roots of "decision-making".

What is a decision?

From an etymological standpoint, "decide" is close to words like homicide, genocide or pesticide, in that they all share a common Latin ending "cide", which means "to kill". De-cide literally means to "kill off alternate choices". When we decide, we pick one option from many. The option we choose gets to "live", while the others don't, therefore they die off.

By making a decision we are willing to let the other possibilities go in favour of the one we think is the best. It's a process of elimination.

So how, then, do we make this assessment? What do we consider to evaluate an option? An analytical way to look at this would be to say our best option is the one that maximises the outcome and minimises the inputs—kind of like the way we choose to make a financial investment and hope to gain.

Of course, everyone has a different interpretation of what is valuable to them, which influences their decision-making, but we can still classify these criteria into "currencies". The most standard ones are indeed money and time. Other valuable but less striking currencies are social status, popularity, energy and wellbeing.

We use these currencies to invest. They represent our inputs, the chips we put on the decision table at the casino of life. And we expect to retrieve more of them (or transform them) as outcomes of our decisions.

We might, for instance, practise a sport like basketball to exercise and connect with new people. So, we are investing time and energy to get wellbeing. We could even invest more time and energy, with the hopes to be good enough to be drafted in the NBA and get paid to play.

When we make decisions, we trade currencies. And overthinking routinely occurs when we are confronted with the equivalent of a big trade with high stakes.

For example, take choosing a university. This is a massive investment of time and money. And obviously, we want the best return possible on our investment. These large trade deals are the decisions we consider important because their repercussions on our lives can be massive.

These are consequential decisions.

And, as opposed to the previous chapter, we are not overthinking the direct outcomes of an opportunity but their ripple effects. When facing high-stakes decisions, like a career move, a house purchase or leaving a partner, we most often perform second-order thinking. We go beyond the immediate outcome of our decision and ask ourselves, "*And then what?*"

The answers are complex, if not convoluted, and we can fall into one of the traps of overthinking, pondering countless scenarios, going down several orders of consequences—all of this stemming from the consequential decisions that need to be made.

Yet, when interviewing overthinkers, it appears that having experience with decision-making, however small, removes some of the uncertainties around the decision-making process and reduces overthinking.

For example, if you've already emigrated to two different countries, you would be less anxious about moving once again to another country than someone who has never done it before. Or, if you've already bought three homes, you are less affected when purchasing your next home than if you are a first-time buyer.

And one of the reasons experience is so impactful is that it grants us the ability to see how to "reverse" a decision.

When first-time expatriates tell themselves they need to spend at least five years in the new country, experienced people know that if they don't like the country they are moving to, they can still come "home" or move somewhere else entirely.

When first-time homebuyers think they will live in the current property for the rest of their lives, experienced people know that they can sell it and buy a new one if they realise they would be better in another place.

What seems irreversible to a first-timer is perceived as reversible with more experience. We know it because we have already done it. We already went through these "reversions". We made a decision, got an outcome, recognised it didn't suit us, so we went back on it. Or we could say we reversed our decision.

Act Before You overThink

Every decision is reversible.

The only exception to this rule is death. Apart from that, every other decision can be reversed. But this operation comes with a price tag attached.

Don't like the new house and regret leaving your previous one? Sell your place and make an offer the new owner of your old home cannot refuse.

Don't enjoy life as an expatriate? Break your housing contract, resign from your current position and leave your adopted country.

Of course, this is not going to be cheap. It will cost time, money, energy, maybe even social status and wellbeing. It was never said that the cost of reversion is always affordable. But if you absolutely want to, you can put the toothpaste back in its tube. It's just freaking hard.

So, even if most decisions can be reversed, practically speaking they are irreversible decisions. These are the ones for which we cannot pay the cost of reversion.

Often people see an irreversible decision as a one-way door. We go through the door and, as it closes, we realise we cannot open it again to return to the other side. It is a one-way trip. Inversely, reversible decisions are perceived as a revolving door, where we freely pass from one side to the other.

But we should update this interpretation and instead see the door as a toll gate. Every time we cross it, there is a cost attached. And sometimes, the cost might be too damn high to pay again!

So, when we look at the decision we have to make, we can categorise it using two criteria: importance and reversibility. If it is important, it means the outcomes are consequential. If it is reversible, it means the outcomes are alterable. And the opposites are, respectively, trivial and permanent outcomes.

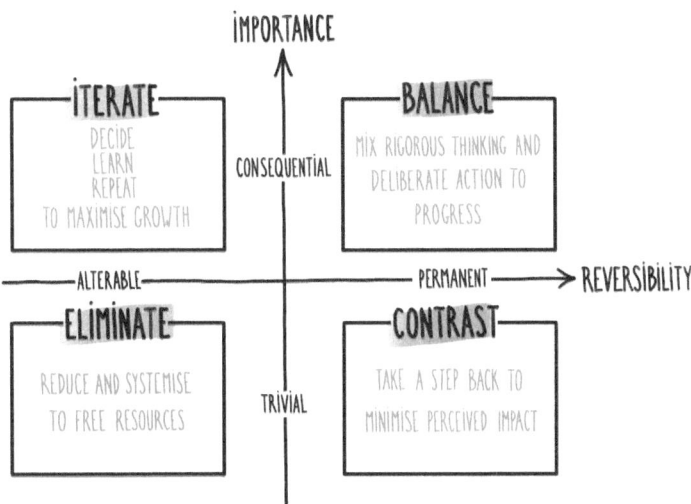

This creates a two-by-two matrix that I named the PACT Decision Matrix, that offers a simple framework to analyse our decisions. Our second filter, the reversibility filter, uses this matrix. For each quadrant, we can find a specific and reliable course of action.

First, let's look at decisions with alterable and trivial outcomes. These constitute the bulk of the decisions we make every day. The little things, like, should we go to the gym? What should we wear today? Which movie should we watch now?

According to a research study conducted by Cornell University, we make more than 200 decisions (conscious and unconscious) that relate to food alone every single day[1].

Obviously, for most of us, none of these choices are life-defining moments. Their impact is limited, so is their importance. Plus, the cost of reversing these decisions is almost negligible, so we can easily alter them. Nonetheless, when constantly accumulated, they can lead to decision fatigue, a psychological phenomenon that impairs our decision-making abilities.

Researchers found that the more choices people had to make at the mall for their shopping, the worse they would perform on simple arithmetic calculations[2]. Additionally, other tests found that the more decisions we make, the more inclined we are to avoid upcoming decisions and procrastinate.

So, we should keep the amount of "trivial – alterable" decisions as low as possible to ensure our brains have the resources to work through more challenging opportunities. And this might require us to "eliminate" some of the decisions we find ourselves making over and over again. A way to do so is to go back to our previous freedom filter and use a process to cut through these decisions.

One system is by implementing "decisions rules". For instance, we establish a rule never to have dessert (it's a harsh one, I agree). Then, when the question comes at a dinner party, we don't have to deliberate; our answer is an automatic "no". Note that this method loses all its power if you start adding exceptions. If the rule is "*I cannot have dessert unless I exercise*", then when we face the decision to have dessert or not, we need to examine whether or not we exercised "enough" to warrant indulgence. So, this leads to having to make another decision, which defeats the purpose of this technique.

One of the rules that I picked up during my engineering studies is always to lock my computer for security reasons while I am away from it. Even at home, even if this is just for a few minutes, it has become an automatic decision.

In addition to decision rules, we can also have routines that simplify daily life. For example, we can decide in advance which clothes we wear for each day of the workweek, or we can limit ourselves to one type of apparel. Steve Jobs adopted this routine, always wearing what seemed to be the same black turtleneck, blue jeans and white sneakers. Likewise, when in office, Barack Obama decided only to wear grey or blue suits to cut through the number of decisions he had to make every day.

Trading up Decisions Reversibility

Then, the second type of decision has trivial and permanent outcomes. The impact of these decisions on our lives is minor but is perceived as definitive. We cannot or, most often, are not willing to pay for the cost of reversion.

Imagine you go to the restaurant, order a dish, and as you are getting served, you realise you made a mistake and wanted something else. You could reverse this decision, but are you willing to bear the cost? Do you see yourself awkwardly explaining to the waiter you want something else? Can you withstand his judgement? You might also have to pay for two dishes and wait an extra 20 minutes. Most of us wouldn't reverse our decision in this case, even if we were currently unhappy with our outcomes, because the cost to be paid would be perceived as a loss which then is associated with regrets and dissatisfaction.

In an attempt to avoid "lose-lose" situations as much as possible, we fall for the status quo bias. Behavioural scientists and economists define this heuristic as an irrational preference for our current situation[3]. Essentially, what we have done, bought into or subscribed to becomes a reference point from which we judge the outcomes of our following choices. And this bias will skew our decision-making process, encouraging us to remain in our comfort zone, only doing what we already know or tried, and completely ignoring the potential benefits of change.

Like when offered the daily special by the waiter, we stuck to the dishes we already had had and liked in this restaurant.

We don't want to risk picking a new dish that would not taste as good as what we are used to eating in this restaurant. It happens at the hairdresser's too. We stick with the same haircut, fearing being disappointed by novelty.

Our bias for the status quo occurs everywhere and every day.

A small town in Germany had to be relocated due to a large mining project. The government was covering the costs of this move to a nearby valley, and specialists suggested several town planning options to the inhabitants. The townspeople selected a layout remarkably similar to the one they were used to in their old town[4].

So, under the influence of the status quo bias, we end up eliminating the decision, but we also miss out on new discoveries and new learnings. As a kid, I used to dislike dark chocolate. It was too bitter for me. But now, as a grown-up, I absolutely love it. I would have missed out on many blissful moments if I had never tried it again.

To mitigate the effects of cognitive bias pushing us to discard new alternatives due to the fear of regrets, we can use "contrast". Basically, we use consequential decisions to put in perspective the trivial ones. It helps us take a step back and re-evaluate the impact of a potential loss in the grand scheme of things. Is it that big a deal to try a new dish and not like it? Who's never experienced a bad haircut once in their life?

And when we look at trivial decisions, we can see them as a "tap" (Trivial – Alterable – Permanent) where we can regulate their flow and intensity through elimination and contrasting techniques.

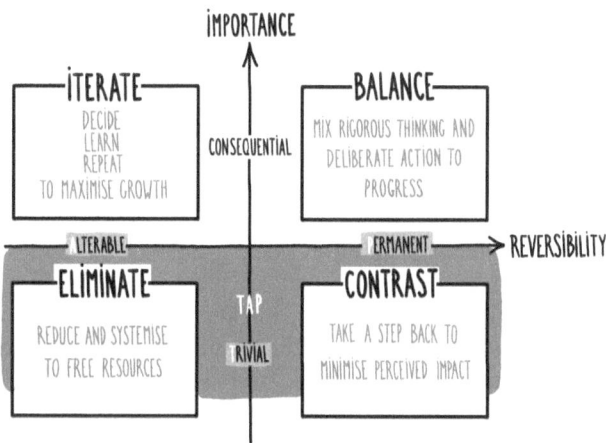

In the same way we turn on and off the tap, we can better manage our mental resources to use them for our consequential decisions. These decisions are more complex and cognitively demanding. As a result, they often make us overthink. They are challenges that require us to pass a "cap" (Consequential – Alterable – Permanent).

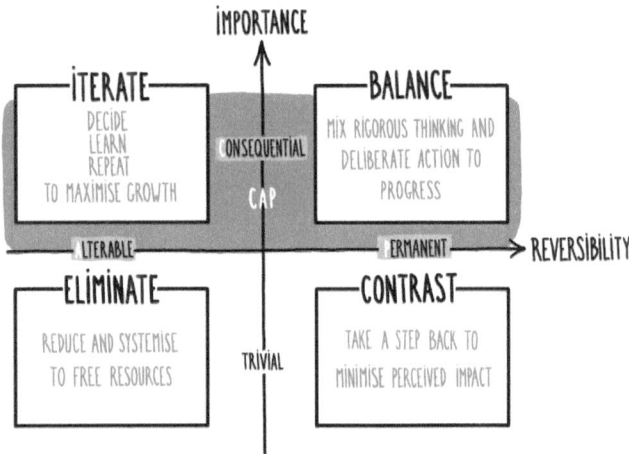

"Consequential – alterable" decisions have a profound impact on us, but at the same time, their cost of reversion is affordable. Although the threshold will vary for each of us, these opportunities are bargains that we should definitely seize. As they have consequential outcomes, we have a lot to learn from them. At the same time, they are alterable, meaning we can revert them if we don't like the results. Plus, there is also the possibility of obtaining excellent outcomes.

In these conditions, it makes sense to "iterate". Although this term is most often used for product development, it conveys an interesting notion that we can leverage for our personal development.

Iterate means to perform repeatedly. And so, we want to make "consequential – alterable" decisions regularly. We should not be afraid of them as they can be reversed. We learn faster by doing them and judging their consequences than by spending weeks over-analysing them.

Trading up Decisions Reversibility

On the contrary, "consequential – permanent" decisions should be dealt with more delicately. When the stakes are high, and there is no way back, it is only natural to slow the pace and take some time to reflect.

In the ancient times when Rome was still a Republic, the consul Julius Caesar waged war in Gaul to increase his wealth and, first and foremost, bolster his reputation. His numerous victories granted him this and even more. Moreover, his troops' indefectible loyalty and his soaring popularity made him a fearsome threat to the Roman Senate, which mandated Caesar to disband his armies and return to Rome.

As he stood on the bank of the Rubicon River, marking the border from Gaul and Italy, the commander had to make a difficult choice. Following orders, risking being exiled, incarcerated or even killed as he had become too menacing for the Republic. Or marching on Rome with his men, committing treason and plunging his homeland into a civil war. There is little doubt that the soon-to-be emperor thought extensively before making this "permanent and consequential" decision. However, he didn't let his thoughts paralyse him either. Once the time for reflection was up, he acted.

As we approach these intense and life-changing decisions, it is essential to balance thinking and doing. Following his "thinking" time, the commander acted and crossed the Rubicon. He could also have sent a messenger saying he was surrendering and returning to Rome— if he thought it was better for him. The point being, Caesar balanced thinking and doing, which led him to keep control over his destiny. Had he thought for too long, the decision would have been made for him. His opponents could have seen his absence of communication as refusing to back down and thus a war declaration.

A modern example could be choosing between two houses. If we wait for too long, one of the owners could accept the offer from another buyer, and the decision would be made for us. As a consequence, we should balance reflection and action when we approach "consequential – permanent" decisions to remain in control of our destiny.

As we covered the two types of consequential decisions, you might wonder how to differentiate? Or, more precisely, what these "consequential – alterable" decisions could be?

For most of us, it is difficult to decorrelate the importance and the irreversibility of decisions. We have this conception that it is most likely to be permanent if it is consequential. Decisions like, "*Should I quit this job?*", "*Should I buy another house?*" or "*Should I marry this person?*" are pretty impactful and also seem pretty hard to undo. We do not naturally come up with answers such as, "*If this doesn't work out, I can still divorce and marry someone else.*"

So, is there such a thing as "consequential – alterable" decisions? Alterable and permanent decisions exist on a continuum. The cursor is determined by the cost of reversion, which varies based on the reversal state you aim for.

Obviously, if you quit your job to start a business, and the move doesn't work out as you expected, you are unlikely to get your old job back. It is not impossible, but you could have to accept a lower wage or bear with the office's gossip surrounding your comeback. In this case, the cost of reversion is high. But if you quit your job to start a business, and when you realise it doesn't work out, you decide to find another job opportunity, the cost of reversion is suddenly much lower. The reversal states are different, but so are their costs.

Additionally, what might have appeared permanent because we could not or were unwilling to pay for the reversion a few years ago might be an obvious necessity now. As you are pondering a marriage proposal, the idea of ever divorcing seems far-fetched. But after years of marriage and feeling miserable, it could be an acceptable solution.

So the cost of reversion is significantly influenced by how we think about it, and sometimes our reflection can be biased. Among the different cognitive biases that affect our judgement, two directly influence our evaluation of the cost of reversion.

Trading up Decisions Reversibility

The first one is loss aversion, which occurs before our decision is made. Basically, we tend to feel a loss more acutely than the equivalent value gain. Let's say we lose 100 dollars; the loss would make us unhappier than the satisfaction we would gain by winning 100 dollars. In fact, the emotional intensity of losing 100 dollars would be the same as winning 200 dollars. Psychologically, losses weigh us down twice as much as gains bring us satisfaction[5]. So then, when we evaluate our cost of reversion before our decision, loss aversion will twist our assessment. It will accentuate the perceived price to be paid and skew our decision-making.

The second bias is the sunk cost fallacy, which takes place after the decision. We invested in our opportunity, turning it into a decision, creating sunk costs. Since we don't want our investment to be wasted, we are more likely to persevere with an endeavour than reverse it, even if it is actually not in our best interest[6].

That's why we stay in the same job expecting a promotion we work so hard for when it would be easier to apply to another company. That's why we keep funding the renovation of an old house, even if it would be cheaper to buy a new one. That's why we stay with our partner of 30 years whom we don't love anymore because we spent so much time together.

This is the sunk cost fallacy at work. We have spent some of our currencies that cannot be recouped, and even if the situation continues to degrade, we don't want to cut our losses. Because of the investment already made with the decision, the sunk cost fallacy distorts our calculation of the cost of reversion.

The exciting part about these cognitive biases is that we can leverage them for our benefit. We can learn to "trade up" irreversibility and turn permanent decisions into alterable ones, which can ease our decision-making process when the high stakes paralyse us. To do so, we need to reduce our cost of reversion.

One way is to share perspectives by hiring a red team. This concept emerged first in the military sphere but is now commonly used by corporations. And we can also use it in our personal life. The red team is in charge of bringing another perspective to our plan, to our decisions. More specifically, the red team challenges assumptions and exposes information we have neglected or inflated[7]. It's there to dismiss any shortcomings or blind spots. It helps to see things differently, from another angle.

In 1954, psychology professors Hastorf and Cantril demonstrated a similar phenomenon with their famous case study *They Saw A Game*, where students from Dartmouth and Princeton Universities saw the exact same football match, opposing their respective teams, but drew completely different conclusions[8]. The game was rough, full of penalties and injuries on both sides, but Princeton students clearly identified Dartmouth players as the aggressors. And the Dartmouth students saw the exact opposite. The reason for this discrepancy? We filter information and weigh it differently than other people, based on many criteria and personal interpretations. That's why the red team concept is powerful. It can reduce our focalism and broaden our reflection.

For example, when contemplating the consequential decision to quit our corporate job to start a coffee business, part of the cost of reversion is the fear of not going back to corporate. Since it creates a gap in our resume, we could think that future recruiters might disregard our application. But our red team, which could be our friends or family, shines more light on this belief. They can remind us we will learn new skills from this experience, which could be valuable to a company. Recruiters can appreciate the specific mindset and values showcased by an individual choosing to start a business. Ultimately, this venture could also push us to meet new people and create opportunities we cannot even imagine now. And adding all these elements from our red team lowers our evaluation of the cost of reversion.

Taking small steps is a second technique we can use to influence our cost of reversion. It requires breaking a permanent decision into a succession of alterable ones. The objective is to reduce our sunk costs to make it easier to reverse our decision, like dipping your toes in first to test the water instead of jumping in all at once.

Instead of quitting our job straight away to start our coffee business, we can take a small step and start to train as a barista every Saturday. This allows us to see if we like working in a coffee job and if the reality matches our expectations. If we don't like it, our corporate job is still there, and we can easily reverse our decision. We can also combine it with a variation of the red team technique, where we reach out to business owners to get their feedback on running this kind of venture to highlight some of our blind spots or inaccurate assumptions. It might even open more "small steps" opportunities, like taking some equities in an already existing and financially healthy coffee shop.

And if turning permanent decisions into alterable ones benefits us, so does the contrary. Two professors from Harvard University and MIT conducted an interesting experiment about the reversibility of decisions. Students in a photography course had to take several meaningful photos, then print two. Then they were told they could only keep one of the two pictures. But half of the group was told they could change their minds within the next few days, whereas the other half knew their decision was irreversible. The results show that those who could change their minds liked the print they selected less. With the ability to reverse their decisions, they were less satisfied with their choice and showed lower levels of happiness and wellbeing than the second group[9].

Although we anticipate reversibility to make us feel better about our decisions, it can surprisingly be the contrary. So forcing a decision to be irreversible can help us. Specifically, when we make a consequential decision, we can be tempted to reverse it before we reach the outcome. We are halfway through crossing a bridge and suddenly get cold feet. What if we don't like it on the other side of the river? What if this is nothing like we envisioned? Would it be safer to turn back? When the results of our decisions are not immediate, we can start overthinking them, imagining all the negative ones (rather than the positive ones).

Consequently, if the decision is alterable, it is quite tempting to reverse it. Like sending a text asking someone out, and before they have the time to answer (or even see our message), we write down, "*Sorry, wrong number.*" But objectively, paying for the cost of reversion without reaching an outcome is a poor decision and a bad move.

To avoid this, I like to borrow a famous piece of wisdom from the *Star Wars* character Yoda that bluntly states, "*Do. Or do not. There is no try.*" Trying is irrelevant. We decide and then do it, or we decide not to and don't do it.

During an exchange with a woman at one of his personal development workshops, motivational speaker Tony Robbins asked her what her intent was. She told him she was trying to fix her marriage. To which he answered, "*Okay, now please stand up and try to grab the chair.*" She followed the command, standing up and grabbing the chair. And Robbins said, "*No, you are not trying! You are grabbing the chair.*" Perplexed, the woman let go of the chair, staying still. "*Well, now you are not grabbing the chair, but you are still not trying.*" The point is that we are not trying something out, we are doing a test. It requires us to set our minds to it. Once decided, we follow through. We are committed.

And one way to force this commitment is to burn bridges. Throughout history, many military exploits have relied on this tactic. During the conquest of Mexico, the Spanish commander Hernán Cortés sunk his troop's ships so that retreat would not be an option anymore[10]. As they could not go back, their only option was to fight and prevail. Like crossing a river and burning the bridge, there is no way back.

In our case, we ensure there is no reversion possible when the cost to pay is prohibitive. And to increase it, we can intensify our loss aversion, making an additional financial commitment, like a bet with a friend. We can also use peer pressure to act as a form of accountability. For instance, we could tell our inner circle that we have decided to quit our job and start a coffee business. As we make a verbal commitment to others, we would lose more in social status if we were to renounce our decision.

Ultimately, the ability to influence the cost of reversion is an incredible skill for decision-making. Consequently, when facing an opportunity, we can use our reversibility filter and ask ourselves if we can trade up reversibility. We reduce its cost to diminish our doubts, easing our choice, or increase it to ensure we are fully committed and, in the end, more satisfied.

◆◆◆◆◆

Zoe contacts Naomie, an alumnus of one of the universities she shortlisted. Without any filter, she explains her difficulties in making such an important choice, and the stress and constant loop of thoughts it creates.

Naomie tells the young woman that she completely understands her. She went through the same process about two decades ago and agrees that this decision significantly impacts her future, but she also highlights how it is not definitive.

Zoe is a bit confused. Once she makes her choice, there is no going back. She will go to one university, refusing the two others. And she will pay the tuition fees. If she doesn't like it there, it is not like she will be refunded.

"You are right, yet this is not as rigid as you might think."

If the courses don't suit her, it is possible to get an equivalence of credits and change the course of her studies. Likewise, if she doesn't like the university, there are often ways to be transferred into another one, through partnership. Zoe appreciates the remarks, realising she didn't think of these possibilities before.

As she thinks about these new elements, Naomie adds, *"You can always change. Nothing is truly irreversible."*

Key Takeaways

- When we make decisions, we trade currencies like time for money. We invest some currencies to either retrieve more of them (or transform them) as outcomes of our decisions.
- Overthinking routinely occurs when we are confronted with "consequential" decisions requiring a large investment of currencies, like purchasing a house or choosing a university.
- Overthinking also occurs when decisions appear to be "permanent", namely the decision is irreversible and its outcomes are definitive.
- But all decisions, with the exception of death, are reversible. However, there is a cost to be paid for the reversion, and practically, decisions are irreversible when we cannot pay this cost.
- Importance and Reversibility criteria form a 2x2 matrix of decision—The PACT Decision Matrix—offering a framework to ease decision-making.
- We should eliminate decisions with "alterable - trivial" outcomes to free our mental bandwidth for other decisions.
- We should contrast decisions with "permanent - trivial" outcomes with decisions with "consequential" outcomes to reduce the status-quo bias and try new things.
- We should iterate decisions with "alterable - consequential" outcomes to foster our personal growth.
- We should balance thinking and doing when making decisions with "permanent-consequential" outcomes to ensure we have enough time to reflect and don't wait too long, so the decision is made for us.
- The reversibility filter can be summarised by the question, "Can I modify the reversibility of my choice to my benefit?"

How-To

When we are facing "consequential" decisions, we can influence its reversibility to help us.

We can trade up irreversibility, turning a permanent decision into an alterable one. It eases our decision-making process and reduces our overthinking. To make this trade, we need to decrease the cost of reversion.
- We can hire a red team to get another perspective on our decision, highlight our blind spots and challenge our assumptions.
- We can take "small steps", breaking the permanent decision into several alterable ones.

We can trade up reversibility, turning an alterable decision into a permanent one. It makes us committed to reaching an outcome and improves our satisfaction after making the decision. To make this trade, we need to increase the cost of reversion.
- To increase the perceived cost of reversion, we can leverage our cognitive biases, such as loss aversion.
- We need to increase the "currencies" invested. The obvious one is the financial aspect, but we can also leverage others, like social status.
- For instance, we can commit to our family verbally about our decision, creating accountability and peer pressure.

To go further, visit lisonmage.com website or directly scan the QR code. You will find additional resources, including downloadable documents, exercises and videos, to help you *Act Before You overThink*.

Chapter 9

Thriving With Core Values

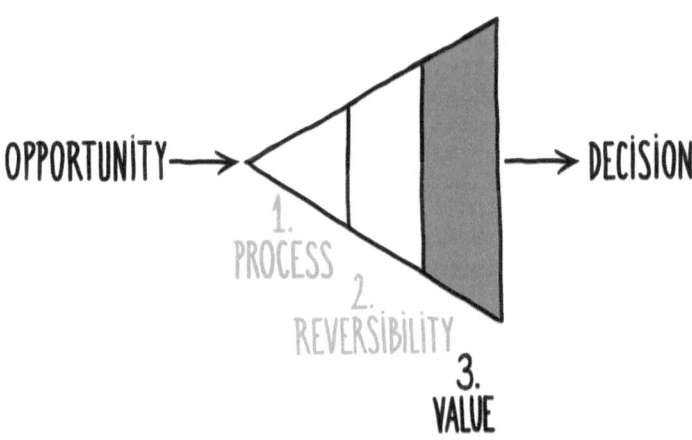

"When your values are clear to you, making decisions becomes easier."

Roy E. Disney

Damian has been working for the last three years as technical lead and project manager for a public company, leading a 17-person team of software engineers. The team has achieved great results under his management, and it didn't go unnoticed. As a result, there are talks about expanding the team, almost doubling its size and giving him a promotion.

At the same time, he has been approached by Judith, a former colleague at the previous company he worked for. She launched her startup two years ago, and its growth has been astronomical. Already on their third round of funding, they secured close to 15 million dollars to accelerate the development of their innovative software technology. However, even if she hired a bunch of smart people, she now needs someone with experience to professionalise their product and improve their internal processes.

She offers Damian the role of Chief Technology Officer and to lead all the technical aspects of her company. On top of providing a significant number of shares, Judith is also ready to match his current salary. Indeed, Damian is flattered by the proposition and asks for a bit of time to think about it.

Out of respect for his current manager Paula, he opens up to her about the startup opportunity. She thanks him for confiding in her and tells him that the company will absolutely make a counter-offer if he waits a bit. Less than 24 hours later, Damian has it in his mailbox. This is a huge promotion, with a massive salary increase and an extended scope of work.

From his point of view, both opportunities look outstanding, and he is clueless about which one to choose.

Some choices seem impossible to make. These are decisions where everyone has an opinion but still says, "*Ultimately, it's your choice,*"

leaving us more perplexed than enlightened. And no matter how we look at our options, we are unable to decide.

This situation is reminiscent of many romantic movies, where the main character finds herself in a bind when both lovers propose, and choosing one means turning down the other. We watch her struggle to decide while rooting for her happiness. But surprisingly, the protagonist most often doesn't have to make the choice by herself; external events out of her control resolve this. The scenario magically leads to a cheerful resolution.

Unfortunately though, when it comes down to our own hard choices, no invisible force pushes us towards a solution that ensures we will "live happily ever after". We are not mere spectators but directors of our life. We are in charge of writing the script, and like any author, we can struggle to find out what to make happen next.

So, what should we do when we face a hard choice?

First, it is worth considering what constitutes a hard choice to answer this question. There are evident examples like choosing between different fields of study or expatriating. But what about having to decide between two desserts, like a crème brûlée or a chocolate fondant? For those with a sweet tooth like me, the choice is tough. One of the biggest misconceptions about hard decisions is that they are not necessarily consequential, such as making a career move. And the opposite is also true; namely, consequential decisions are not always hard decisions.

A decision is easy when there is a clear winner among all our alternatives. One solution stands out and looks like the obvious one to pick. It could be that buying your first house or marrying is an easy decision, even if this is—at the same time—a consequential one. On the contrary, a hard choice means no apparent option rises above all else.

According to Dr Chang, a professor at the University of Oxford, hard choices cannot be rationalised with scientific measurements[1]. To conduct her demonstration, she assumes that comparing two hard decisions is like comparing the weight of two suitcases. When we do so, there are only three possible outcomes. The first suitcase is heavier, lighter or has the same weight as the second suitcase. If we apply the same reasoning to our decision, the first option would be better, worse or equal to the second option. Then, the conclusion would be that a hard decision only offers alternatives of equal value.

In Damian's case, both options seem equally good, which is why he is hesitant and struggling to choose. Yet, if this is true, then slightly improving one proposal would be enough to make it better than the other, and then his choice would be a "no-brainer". For instance, if Damian's company decides to improve their offer by increasing his annual salary package by a few hundred dollars, this should tip the balance in one direction and make the company's offer better than the startup's one. But in reality, this is unlikely to change anything. Even with this offer's improvement, Damian would still be undecided.

Consequently, a decision is hard, not because its options are of equal value, but because they are in the same range of value.

The reason why we cannot precisely evaluate these options is due to the fact that there are intangible elements we cannot quantify. For instance, how much would wellbeing matter? How can we accurately compare the job satisfaction the two options would provide? It becomes even more complex if we try to gauge wellbeing against other criteria such as growth or the future opportunities that result from our choice. The only conclusion we can arrive at is that the options presented by a hard decision seem roughly equal. Professor Chang named the alternatives as being "on a par".

Hard decisions we perceive as impossible dilemmas only offer options on a par. And when we can't find a clear winner, we doubt and overthink. After all, if we are truly blind to which option is better and logic cannot help us decide, then choosing is purely at random.

It is as if, when facing a hard decision like choosing between two job opportunities or two lovers, the best thing to do is flip a coin to make up our mind.

Indeed it seems insane to let luck choose for us, but it is actually a good test to find out if two options are on a par. If we flip a coin and immediately experience a strong feeling of relief or unease based on the outcome, it strongly indicates that we prefer one option over the other, meaning they are not on a par.

However, this mind trick might not work because we are truly facing a hard decision. In this case, we should examine one of the most renowned ethical problems—the trolley dilemma—to help choose without foolishly leaving our future up to chance.

The thought experiment places us close to a train track junction. As we hear a train approaching at full speed, we realise five railway workers are on its path. However, even if they notice a threat is approaching, they would not have the time to escape it. Searching for solutions, we find a lever we can pull that would divert the train onto a second set of tracks, saving them. But as we are about to activate it, we realise there is a lone worker on the second path, and he seems to be as oblivious as his colleagues. If we pull the lever, we are condemning him to death. But if we do nothing, the other five will be killed.

What would you do?

Would you pull the lever, saving five lives for the price of one? Or would you decide not to interfere, letting the five workers meet their end? Is there a "best" or even simply a "right" answer to this dilemma? Even if this ethical problem is unrealistic and purely theoretical, we can learn from its answers and their implications.

One approach is utilitarianism, a theory the English philosopher Jeremy Bentham was a proponent of. He was famous for saying "the greatest happiness for the greatest number", and believed that our decisions should always aim to optimise this principle. Basically, we should analyse the situation with a focus on the consequences of our actions in order to minimise pains and maximise gains[2].

If we do nothing in the trolley dilemma, five people will die. But if we pull the lever, only one will. As a consequence, saving five lives at the expense of one, although terrible, appears to be the most acceptable solution because it achieves the highest level of utility.

On the opposite side, we find deontology, a philosophical approach supported by the German philosopher Immanuel Kant. His theory of ethics has a set of rules to determine whether an act is morally acceptable. One of these imperatives requires not using people as a "means to an end"[3].

And in the trolley dilemma, when we compare the weight of five lives against one, we break this rule. We are objectifying human life by judging which life is more valuable. After all, who are we to decide five lives are worth more than one? What if these are five criminals serving life sentences saved for the price of a young child? Where do we set the thresholds? The deontological answer is that we cannot decide what is acceptable or not because we cannot and should not quantify the value of each individual. Thus, we should never pull the lever.

Researchers conducted a study with more than 70,000 participants in 42 countries to test how they would respond when confronted with the trolley dilemma[4]. Interestingly, they found significant cultural differences.

In the Western countries, including the USA and Europe, about 85% of respondents would adopt a utilitarian view, flipping the switch to save five individuals and killing one, choosing "the lesser evil".

However, in Eastern countries, including China and Japan, only 70% decided to pull the lever. When the surveyors asked the participants that chose not to interfere to justify their choice, they often explained that they didn't have the right to make this decision, which aligns more with Kantian ethics[5].

These findings highlight an essential conclusion of the trolley dilemma. This hypothetical situation has no correct answer. Yet, people follow what they feel is right when pushed to decide. They make their decisions based on their values.

The lesson from this Cornelian dilemma is that we all have our own set of values built over time from our environment and experiences that can assist us, even unconsciously, when confronted with hard decisions, hence why our last freedom filter is the value filter. Values we stand by help us navigate these impossible decisions with alternatives on a par.

When we find out what our values are and use them as the highest driver for our decisions, we know why we do things. It is one of the critical ideas detailed by Simon Sinek in his book *Start With Why*. He argues that we should focus on why, which is at the core of our decisions and actions, before we get to how and finally what. By asking why we are doing something, it not only brings us clarity, it fosters our determination and compels us to act. Then, it becomes tremendously easier to go through the questions of how and what.

According to Sinek, companies should always start with why as it unveils what they stand for, what their values are and ultimately enable them to create an emotional connection with their prospects. For example, Harley Davidson doesn't sell us motorcycles. Instead, it sells us freedom: the long rides on desert roads with the sunset on our backs. And if this value resonates with us, it will create a stronger bond with the brand. We are not buying a product anymore but an experience that reflects our convictions.

Leaders, aiming to inspire us, do the same. They start with why. They talk to our identity using our values to create a deeper connection and galvanise us. And as we are the leaders of our life, it is fundamental to focus on our why, uncover our values and build our convictions. It allows us to filter alternatives on a par and find the one that resonates the most with who we are and want to be. Then, we don't have to ask ourselves if we should do something, we'll simply know it because we understand what is truly important to us.

But finding what our core values are and ranking them is no small feat.

As he tries to compare both opportunities, Damian wonders what he values the most.

Is stability indispensable to him? His current company offers this, but the startup option might be lacking in this area.

At the same time, joining Judith might be a bolder challenge. The rhythm will be completely different to what he has experienced in his professional life so far. After all, working at startups means you take on responsibilities that go far beyond your job description. Although he always considered himself a hard-working person, he knows he will have to go through massive ups and downs. Is he really this adventurous?

Also, his current company has always been good to him. They trusted and empowered him—that certainly must count for something. Isn't he a loyal person?

◆◆◆◆◆

Establishing our values and ranking their significance is a profound exercise in self-discovery. It is initially puzzling and requires an introspective exploration.

At first, it can be scary to look inward and question ourselves, like going into a dark basement. We slowly go down the stairs with our torch, wondering what we will find there. We can be frightened by the shadows, mistaking them for monsters, but once we turn on the light, we realise their true nature. And then we find some boxes full of blissful memories.

Oftentimes, we refrain from asking questions. It doesn't matter if they are straightforward or profound, we push them back, judging them as silly. Who wants to go to the basement anyway? There's nothing down there but a bunch of old and useless stuff.

Throughout our life, we encounter so many external signs and behaviours which mentally condition us to ignore questions or stop questions. It could have been taught by our parents with their sighs of exasperation or rolling their eyes when we repeated a question. It could have been taught when we got mocked for raising our hands at school. It could have been taught at work by the disdainful smirk of our colleagues when we wondered why we were doing things the way we were.

Fearing the judgement of others, we somehow unconsciously learn to stop asking questions. We don't want to appear stupid in the moment. But if we remain silent, we will be stupid forever. So, in reality, the only "wrong" questions are the ones we don't ask.

But what to do if no one can answer our questions? When it comes to our values, this is so personal that parents, teachers and mentors can only provide hints and pieces of wisdom to guide us. So to get a clear response, we have to figure it out by ourselves.

And the first step to doing so is to be curious. The rover sent to Mars in 2011, which explored the Red Planet for more than six years, was named Curiosity. When submitting this name to NASA, twelve-year-old Clara Ma explained that curiosity is "*our need to ask questions and to wonder,*"[6] helping us push boundaries and expand the world we know of.

But to make discoveries, curiosity alone is not enough. When we ask ourselves a question, we need to have the audacity to look for the answer. Is there water on Mars? Interesting question. That's curiosity. Spending 3.1 billion dollars to send a car-sized robot on a 560-million-km journey through outer space and land in the crater Gale, which might have been an ancient lake[7], four billion years ago—that's audacity!

And this combination of curiosity and audacity shouldn't stop at scientific experiments; it also applies to our interrogations about ourselves.

Together, they help us develop our self-awareness. Psychologist Dr Tasha Eurich defines it as the ability to see ourselves clearly, to be consciously aware of our internal state, such as our emotions, feelings, thoughts, as well as our relationships and interactions with others[8]. Thus, there are two elements to self-awareness: an internal component and an external one. To work on our internal self-awareness, we practise introspection and look inward. For our external self-awareness, we seek feedback.

With curiosity as a starting point, we think and reflect about ourselves. We wonder what our values could be. Then, we audaciously put our findings to the test. And we learn from our actions and the reactions of others. When they are both combined, we end up understanding ourselves better. We become more self-aware and discover what is truly important to us.

It is a journey, a continuous exercise. Our values will change with time because they will be influenced by our life experiences. What we value most in our early adulthood will most likely differ twenty years later. So we have to remain both curious and audacious to reassess our values on a regular basis. This is how we create our value filter. With this freedom filter, we can look at our hard decisions and wonder which one of our options is more aligned with our values. Or if they both meet some of our values, which one fulfils our highest value.

Searching for our highest value can be tricky, especially when we begin to use the value filter. Nonetheless, overthinkers often have a few hints because they are curious by nature. They excel at the introspection part, at asking themselves questions. But they fail to find answers.

Curiosity is only one part of the equation. Without audacity, it is incomplete. We need the audacity to take a leap of faith and act. These actions answer our questions. Maybe their outcomes do not match our expectations. Still, they benefit us as we learn from them and progress in our search for our values. Curiosity guides us to new grounds, and audacity pushes us to play on them.

One practical way to work on both our curiosity and audacity is the "five-minute wonder" daily challenge exercise. Every evening, set an alarm clock at a random time for the next day. And when the alarm clock rings, you pause what you are doing for five minutes and look around yourself. The intent is to notice the unfamiliar in the familiar.

If you are walking in the street, do you notice any intriguing shops? What are they selling? If you are on the bus, what do the people look like? What are they doing? If you are at the office, what is happening outside your office window? In these situations, what is interesting? What is piquing your curiosity? And once you find something intriguing, how do you find out more about it? How do you act audaciously? If you notice a new Thai restaurant in the street, you could make a reservation. If you catch the book title someone is reading on the bus, you could order it or read a summary online. Looking out of the office window, you might see a distant park you have never been to. You could decide to have lunch there.

Thriving With Core Values

The purpose of the challenge is to discover and explore new things we like or dislike. And if what we have discovered brings us joy, excitement and satisfaction, then we might decide it aligns with our values. Or it can make us indifferent, or worse, create a feeling of dissatisfaction, anger or disgust which would indicate we are going against our values. As we uncover more about ourselves and our values, we build a lighthouse to show us the way and guide us in our decisions.

When we face hard decisions, we have to fight doubts, fears and uncertainty. Under the influence of these emotions, we have seen how overthinking leads us on the path of avoidance, procrastination or even resignation. And above all else, we must overcome our inhibition because waiting indefinitely is not an option.

The "Buridan's donkey" philosophical paradox perfectly conveys this last point. The story portrays an ass at an equal distance between two stacks of hay. Both look as tasty and as large as each other. The poor animal battles with a hard decision and doesn't know which pile to eat from. Unable to decide, the donkey remains immobile, in the same spot, and finally dies from hunger. The conclusion is obviously absurd, as no real animal would let itself starve to death, even when confronted with alternatives on a par. However, we can be like the donkey. When we find ourselves in the same situation, undecided, remaining in inertia and passively waiting, we are starving ourselves.

University students in ethics classes are frequently challenged with impossible dilemmas. One of them is presented with the following situation. You are at the head of a Red Cross humanitarian convoy in a country in the midst of civil war. You are heading to one of the most impoverished zones, where the local population doesn't have access to clean water and has almost no food supply. They rely solely on your help to survive the incoming days.

You are stopped by rebels on the way. Seeing the logo on your trucks, the militia chief offers you a deal. You can either return to the capital city with your shipment or safely pass if you accept giving them 20% of your cargo.

Act Before You overThink

The issue? If you accept, the local government could think that your organisation is siding with the insurgents, providing them support under cover of being an NGO. As a consequence, the Red Cross could be permanently banned from the country, everyone's visas revoked and the obligation to leave immediately. It could indefinitely compromise the aid it is providing in the region.

You can decide to go back to the capital with your supplies and try again later, but this would take days, and many would perish without your immediate assistance. Or you could agree to the deal, supplying part of your cargo to the opponents of the regime and saving lives, but risk jeopardising all future operations.

What would you decide?

Like the trolley dilemma, there is no right or wrong answer. If we don't deliver the food, people will die. There is no reversibility there. In comparison, we can still recover the aftermath of dispatching the shipment while giving a portion to the rebels. We can contact authorities to explain the situation and appease their anger. We can organise press conferences to reiterate our neutrality.

Ultimately, it comes down to what we can control and what we can't. We cannot control the reaction from the government, but we can control whether or not people will die and the fallouts of our decisions by taking action.

When facing hard decisions, we should rely on our values to guide us and be biased towards what we can control and act upon.

Pondering over his two opportunities, Damian remains undecided. Both parties have been waiting for his answer for weeks. Judith told him she needed to move forward, and if he didn't give her a response in the coming days, she would have to look for other candidates.

He has to decide now. Otherwise, the decision will be made for him.

Still, he has been using his time wisely, looking back at his work but also life experiences to see what the common thread was and find out what truly mattered to him. And as far back as he can remember, he has always had the desire to learn and expand his knowledge.

Even in his current position, his manager Paula allowed him to explore ideas. They both recognise this was one of the main reasons his team was so successful over the last few years.

Discussing with Judith, he realises that he would not have the same liberty even with the CTO position. Right now, shareholders want the startup to focus on delivering. They need structure and processes, not more exploration.

Damian thought he might be able to start new development projects. But not for now. Judith was quite adamant that this is not part of the deal at the moment as their funding doesn't allow it.

As all these elements click together, his decision appears much more straightforward than he initially thought. He has made up his mind. He will stay with his company and take the promotion—it's more aligned with what he truly aspires to.

Coming to this realisation offers him profound relief. He was scared to miss an opportunity, especially if the startup performs well in future. But now, he is convinced he is making the right decision because he is being true to himself.

Key Takeaways

- Hard decisions are not necessarily consequential decisions. And vice-versa.
- A decision is hard when there is no clear winner among all our options. In this case, options are said to be on a par.
- Options on a par are not of equal value but within the same value range. This is explained by the impossibility of evaluating analytically intangible elements such as wellbeing, growth or future opportunities.
- When we face decisions with options on a par, it can feel like impossible dilemmas. To help us choose, we must find our values.
- When we follow our values, we know why we are doing something and it builds up our conviction and fosters our motivation.
- Finding values requires developing our self-awareness.
- We use curiosity to work on our internal self-awareness, practising introspection. We think and reflect on ourselves, asking questions.
- We use audacity to work on our external self-awareness, seeking feedback. We take action to find answers to our questions.
- The value filter can be summarised by the question: Is it aligned with my values?

How-To

When we feel we are facing a decision with two options on a par and we cannot make up our minds, we can flip a coin. The result can be pretty revealing, indicating if we unconsciously have a preferred option based on our emotional reaction.

We can use the combination of curiosity and audacity to find the values we deeply resonate with. To do so, we can use the daily challenge exercise called the "five-minute wonder".
- Every evening, set an alarm clock at a random time for the next day.
- When the alarm rings, pause what you are doing for five minutes.
- Be curious and look around yourself. Notice the unfamiliar in the familiar
- Once you notice something intriguing, be audacious and find a way to learn more about it.
- As you explore new things, you can create two categories: things you like and dislike.
- Focus on the experiences that bring you joy, excitement and satisfaction as they should highlight some of your values.

Finally, when facing a hard decision:
- Don't be a Buridan's donkey, starving itself to death as it is unable to choose between two haystacks, equally tasty and large.
- Remember, you cannot remain undecided forever or the decision will be made for you.
- Acknowledge what you cannot control, and act upon what you can control.

 To go further, visit lisonmage.com website or directly scan the QR code. You will find additional resources, including downloadable documents, exercises and videos, to help you *Act Before You overThink*.

Conclusion of the Third Myth

Overthinking is only inevitable if we let it be.

If we are prisoners of our own minds, we have to remember we are also our jailers. Somehow, we lost the keys to our liberty in the maze of our thoughts. And we can either sit in the corner of our cell, blaming fate for cursing us. Or we can look for the keys to get out.

Overthinking is a pernicious habit we can fight using mental models. The freedom filters are the key to escape. With them, we can sever the connection between a triggering event and overthinking behaviour. They offer us an efficient way to break down an opportunity and come to a decision by asking ourselves.

- Am I focusing on the outcome instead of the process?
- Can I modify the reversibility of my choice to my benefit?
- Is it aligned with my values?

We can leverage these pragmatic and straightforward questions when we are tempted to overthink our decisions. And one of the most remarkable characteristics of the freedom filters is their adaptability. In this section, we discovered three specific filters: process, reversibility and value. But you can also come up with your own filters. You can choose to use different mental models that you find more suitable for handling your overthinking.

Conclusion of the Third Myth

Regardless, what is essential is understanding the concept of freedom filters and then finding the ones that allow you to overcome the inevitability of overthinking. You must have your mental models readily accessible when you notice a situation that could lead to overthinking. And if you aim to develop your own freedom filters, remember that they are sort of "rules of thumb" and should be summarised with a simple question.

For instance, we could make intuition part of our freedom filters. Intuition is an unconscious cognitive process to obtain knowledge. So we could say that intuition is knowing without knowing how we know[1].

We can see intuition in the genius of a chess master. With a simple glance at the game board, she can predict the number of plays before checkmate.

We can see intuition in the premonition of the firefighter who knows that something is wrong when inside a burning house and evacuates seconds before the building collapses.

But intuition can be a treacherous mistress and mislead us, too. This is why I prefer the revised definition of Nobel-prize winning economist Daniel Kahneman, "Intuition is thinking we know without knowing how we know." Having a high level of confidence based on a gut feeling is not a sign that our intuition is correct. Hence why, when our intuition tells us "*Number 10 will win this horse race,*" we need to add "I think" as in "*I think Number 10 will win this horse race*" to distance ourselves from our prediction and temper an excess of assurance.

According to Kahneman, for intuition to work accurately, there are three specific conditions to comply with[2].

First, we need regularity. Without it, you cannot learn and conclusively extrapolate. Intuition cannot work in a chaotic situation with randomly obtained results, such as the national lottery.

Second, you need a lot of practice. The chess master and the firefighter have dozens of years or more of training. It allows them to unconsciously draw from this accumulated experience to form their intuition.

And finally, you must have immediate feedback. Namely, we quickly know whether or not our decision is right or wrong. For instance, if we make a terrible move on the chessboard, this could soon end the game.

In 2009, right after take-off, US Airways Flight 1549, an Airbus A320, ran into a flock of wild geese and lost both engines. Within seconds, the captain realised the plane could not make it back to their departure airport LaGuardia due to their low altitude, even if it were the recommended procedure. Instead, he chose to perform a water landing, a perilous manoeuvre, in the Hudson River.

Although he successfully landed and saved all passengers, his decision drew much attention. When asked how he knew it was impossible to fly back to LaGuardia, he said he just knew. The captain's intuition was unconsciously formed from his decades of experience, the regularity and immediate feedback of a mental shortcut called the gaze heuristic, enabling him with a glance to know if he can reach a specific place[3].

So, if we adopt intuition as one of our freedom filters, we could be asking ourselves if the opportunity we are facing "feels" right or what our gut says about it. While, at the same time, we remember that to trust our intuition fully, the situation should match the three criteria of regularity, experience and immediate feedback.

Feel free to come up with as many freedom filters as you want, but don't forget one of the rules of value of information from Chapter 1: more is not always best. The most crucial part is that the freedom filters enable you to make decisions easily and efficiently.

Conclusion

Some people suffer from a terrible condition called tinnitus. They constantly hear a sound like a ringing in their ears, even when in complete silence. Its intensity ranges from quiet background whistling to the high-pitched sound of thousands of cicadas buzzing. The condition usually intensifies over time, degrading concentration levels and leading to complications such as anxiety and depression[1].

One of the root causes of tinnitus is a damaged ear that can no longer hear but still tries to process sound, sending phantom noises to the brain. Likewise, overthinking generates excessive thoughts to be processed and produces mental background noise. Both can become unbearable, causing tremendous negative effects.

Unfortunately, nothing cures tinnitus. There is no way to stop the ringing, but this is not the case with overthinking, which can be managed, diminished and defeated.

Overthinking is an excess of thoughts that lead to harmful consequences. And it lives and grows out of three myths we believe. We trust overthinking enhances our thinking, is inconsequential to us and is inevitable in decision-making. As we dispel the myths, we see the true nature of overthinking.

Firstly, overthinking impairs our thinking. Yes, thinking is good, but not when we "over" do it. It is like chocolate mousse—delicious, but it makes us nauseous and disgusted in excess.

Conclusion

Secondly, overthinking is consequential to us. The longer we let a fox in the henhouse, the worse the damages will be. Thus, it is necessary to address this maladaptive behaviour as soon as possible.

Lastly, overthinking is preventable in decision-making. Like any other habit, it can be unlearned without compromising the quality of our choices.

And once we embody these statements, we destroy the foundations from which overthinking can emerge.

Now, you know how to conquer your overthinking. But this is not enough. There is one last and vital point that remains. You must act.

Act before you overthink!

We all know the wise adage, "Think before you act." But I find it incomplete and even misleading for overthinkers, as they can be tempted to remain in contemplation forever. Therefore we should add an extension to the maxim.

Think before you act, but act before you overthink.

Overthinking feeds on an imbalance between thinking and doing. It preys on the limits of our cognition, fuels our deepest fears and creates gripping doubts. But once we act, uncertainty vanishes, taking with it fears and doubts.

Like going for our first skydive. Before jumping, we extensively rehearse on the ground, we know everything about the gears and what they should do during the jump. But when the plane door opens, we freeze, completely paralysed. More thinking is not going to help. To clear doubts and face our fears, we have to jump.

We must act.

Act Before You overThink

Talking with more than 365 overthinkers over a year, I have learned that they are clever and sensible people. However, they let overthinking hinder and prevent them from reaching their full potential.

If you recognise yourself as an overthinker, know you have the power to change! You have an incredible gift to offer to the world.

Imagine what your life would be once freed of overthinking. Imagine what it would feel like to remove this constant background noise for good. So many told me they would feel appeased, liberated, blissful. It is as if you remove an inner weight from your chest, and you can now breathe better. You would be a new self, happier and lighter. And it would impact all the areas of your life.

In your career, it would improve your relationships with your colleagues and smooth your communication. Your productivity and efficiency would improve, freeing your mind for your other activities.

In your personal life, it would enable you to show your true self and feel accepted for who you are. And for the first time, finally be mindful of the present moment, grateful to share it with your loved ones.

Without overthinking, it is the beginning of a new life.

So, take the learnings from this book, think about them and most importantly, act upon them. You have this power within you! And in this quest, remember the fantastic quote from philosopher and author Simone de Beauvoir.

"Change your life today. Don't gamble on the future, act now, without delay."

Working With Me

I wrote this book, for you and others around you, with the aim to raise self-awareness about overthinking and share the keys to overcoming this harmful habit.

Using this book and the additional resources on my website, you have access to a complete framework to guide you in your journey. Yet, every person has a different story and unique challenges. If you need a more dedicated approach, I would love to explore how we can work together on your personal development and growth.

Overthinking also hinders teams' performance. I regularly conduct workshops with leaders, managers and individual contributors to improve wellbeing, increase efficiency and foster a growth mindset. If you would like my help, I'd love to be yours.

Please reach out, share your story and tell me what you think about the book. I would love to have a conversation about how we can work together.

Connect with me: contact@lisonmage.com or
on LinkedIn: https://www.linkedin.com/in/lisonmage

Interview Contributors

- Aarya Raghubanshi
- Abdessamad Hilali
- Abhijeet Kulkarni
- Adam Green
- Adrien Chaigne
- Ailen Wickham
- Ailsa Azizah
- Aishanee Weeraaundara
- Alain Foulon
- Ali Hassan
- Alice Clark
- Alicia Doherty
- Alison Oates
- Allegra Moore
- Alvine Agbo
- Amandine Nury
- Amélie Tranois
- Anaïs Pivin
- Andy Prosser
- Angela Moutinho
- Ann Acaylar
- Anna Doluner
- Anu Thothathri
- Aquila Masri
- Arturo J Galvez
- Ashley Sinkovich
- Ashok Menghani
- Ashwin
- Aslynn Ha
- Asma Brahimi
- Atish Bhana
- Aude Thomasset
- Aurore Tarriere
- Ayoub Mourid
- Baby Nagayo
- Beatriz Ribeiro
- Ben Brand
- Benjamin Plessis
- Berry Zhou
- Bertrand Brudon
- Bich Jennings
- Brian Hankey
- Caleb
- Cassandre DeBonneville
- Cat Moyle
- Cecilia Huang
- Celine Chakhtoura
- Céline Haeck
- Changhui Lu
- Charles Gillman
- Charles-Louis Allizard
- Charm Lupena
- Chiara Seidenman
- Chris Gordon
- Chris Mandis
- Chris Miller
- Christophe Geny
- Christophe Poisson
- Christopher Whitehill
- Cindy Kennedy
- Claudia Putri
- Clément Moliné
- Colette Mason
- Daniella Shelley
- Dario Mratovich
- Darshi McKenzie

Act Before You overThink

- Davette Thompson
- David Fleischmann
- David Saunders
- David Tan
- Deepti Kandhol
- Denise Christie
- Derick Mildred
- Diamond Dong
- Diana Vega Marin
- Didier Comet
- Diya Shivlani
- Dora Zhang
- Dr Bronwyn Evans
- Dr. Riyang Phang
- Duncan Alderson
- Duncan Clark
- Edward Rolfe
- Effie Du
- Elie Bechara
- Elodie Barbera
- Elodie Koeberlé
- Emma Seaman
- Emma Suzanna
- Eric Ye
- Eva Csiki
- Evelyn Tao
- Eyal Wolstin
- Fahad Ahmed
- Faith Tran
- Fernanda Tarabay
- Fiona Murray
- Florian Hivert
- Francois-Xavier Bonnet
- Gaurav Chauhan
- Geoff Wilson
- Geoffrey Ren
- Gisela Renata
- Guillaume Bercier
- Gunnar Habitz
- Guy McPhee
- Hendrix Lando
- Hervé Richard
- Herwig Schiefermüller
- Iain Macleod
- Ian Clarke
- Irene Rodriguez
- Iván Moreno Russi
- James Levin
- Jamie Ezekiel-Hart
- Janice Tong
- Janine Lewinton Dormer
- Jason Levi
- Jason Wellington
- Jeff Bogensberger
- Jeneil Stephen
- Jenni Heino
- Jenny Vaz
- Jeromy Zhu
- Jessica Cruz
- Jessica La Costa
- Jia Keatnuxsuo
- Jianan Lou
- Joanne Fisher
- Joe Greenwood
- Joel Coelho
- Joel Collings

Interview Contributors

- Johanna Waibuca
- Jonathan Becker
- Jonathan Hatchuel
- Josephine Thang
- Joshua Maddux
- Jp B
- Julien Rapinat
- Kareen Vu
- Kasia Bigda
- Kate Harris
- Katrina Hardie
- Kelvin Dao
- Kevin Hayes
- Kevin Tran
- Kim Garretty
- Kim Jerbo
- Klaudia Szygenda
- Kristine Vella
- Kyle Page
- Lana Martin
- Laura Salis
- Laurence Nicole
- Laurent Derache
- Libby Dale
- Lilia Tarlev
- Lilian Wong
- Lisa Ishihara
- Loren De Laine
- Louis Ickx
- Lubica Shannon
- Lucky Sharma
- Maarten Van Den Bos
- Madelyne Cook
- Magali Gendre
- Mai Le
- Manar Khodr
- Maria Victorova
- Marie Curutchet
- Marie Delage
- Marie Fitzgerald
- Marie Tissot
- Marion Brisset
- Mark Ogden
- Marshall Morris
- Marshall Tsien
- Masanori Nakagawa
- Matthieu Flacher
- Mawin Xu
- Maxime Hardy
- Maxime Thuriot
- Meghan Davidson
- Mehdi Heidari
- Melinda-Jane X
- Melissa Vassiliou
- Michael Alderson
- Michael Brooke
- Michael Charbonnier
- Michael Kelly
- Michael Kollo
- Michelle Hancic
- Michelle Licciardi
- Michelle Logan
- Michelle Mcgrane
- Mihir Panchal
- Mike O'Connell
- Moez Bouzayani

Act Before You overThink

- Morgan Chappell
- Mourita Chowdhury
- Nabil Zaim
- Naomi Menahem
- Naseer Taseer
- Natalie Davenport
- Nausica Sala
- Navya B P
- Neha Dhakla
- Noor Aishah Arsad
- Oceane Piaia
- Olivia Zhou
- Olivier Planckeel
- Omar Samadi
- Pascal Delloue
- Patricia Kung
- Patrick Tan
- Paulina Kabaczuk
- Paulo Abreu Vieira da Costa
- Pearl Lee
- Pes Kahawita
- Peter Breusch
- Phoebe Qi
- Phuong Linh Doan
- Pierre Letter
- Pierre-Yves Gerard
- Piyush Mehta
- Prabu Satchithananda
- Pradyut Vatsa
- Pranav Khanna
- Pranav Sharma
- Rafael Porto Carrero
- Raghav Thapar
- Rahul Gori
- Ran Yan
- Robert Marshall
- Robi Karp
- Rodney Edgar
- Sabry Macher
- Sagar Soni
- Sajeeb Lohani
- Sam Karatasas
- Samantha Christie
- Samantha Postman
- San Kulkarni
- Sanaa Ali
- Sandra Blair
- Sarah Lugay
- Sarah Mesloub
- Sarah Wilson
- Sarah Young
- Seline Hardy
- Sewit Tewodemedhin
- Shaun McEwan
- Shineha Radhakrishnan
- Shivam Gupta
- Shrivardhan Kantharia
- Sidonie Winther
- Simon Pavoine
- Siwei Ding
- Sixtine Neufville
- Sofia Balingit
- Solene Lamboley
- Sonny Sharma
- Sri Teja Amam
- Stanley Kan

Interview Contributors

- Steven Bradley
- Steven Whittington
- Su-en Williams
- Sumaiya Tasnim
- Suman Yadav
- Sumit Bhattacharya
- Sweta Tare
- Tantri Das
- Tao Liang
- Tara Dharnikota
- Thomas Oudart
- Tim Kendall
- Tracy De Paolis
- Trami Thai
- Ushan Lokuge
- Ushani Dinushika
- Vanessa Bradbury
- Varsha Nimalendran
- Venessa Kyriakou
- Victor Lebret
- Victoria Gilbert
- Vidya Jadhav
- Viknesvaran Outtandy
- Vincent Bourgarel
- Vincent Liu
- Vincent Ricard
- Vincere Zeng
- Warren Anthony Chu
- Warren Read
- Welland Chu
- Wenlin Jin
- Willa Budiman
- William Kilque
- William Main
- Yang Chen
- Yves Larquemin
- Zakaria Boughalem
- Zeena Skelly

Bibliography

Introduction

1-Ngodup Tenzin et al., "Activity-dependent, homeostatic regulation of neurotransmitter release from auditory nerve fibers," *Proceedings of the National Academy of Sciences* 112 (2015): 6479–6484.

2-Banbury Simon, Berry Dianne C., "Habituation and dishabituation to speech and office noise," *Journal of Experimental Psychology: Applied* 3 (1997): 181–195.

3-Birgitta Berglund, Thomas Lindvall, Dietrich H. Schwela, "Guidelines For Community Noise", *World Health Organisation* (1999).

4-Tobías Aurelio et al., "Health impact assessment of traffic noise in Madrid (Spain)," *Environmental Research* 137 (2015): 136–140.

The First Myth: Overthinking is Enhancing my Thinking

1-Lyubomirsky Sonja et al., "Thinking about rumination: the scholarly contributions and intellectual legacy of Susan Nolen-Hoeksema," *Annual Review of Clinical Psychology* 11 (2015): 1-22.

2-Smith Jeannette M., Alloy Lauren B., "A roadmap to rumination: A review of the definition, assessment, and conceptualization of this multifaceted construct," *Clinical Psychology Review* 29 (2009): 116–128.

3-Deci Edward, Ryan Richard M., *Intrinsic Motivation and Self-Determination in Human Behavior* (Springer, 1985).

Chapter 1

1-Lo Alice, Abbott Maree J., "Review of the Theoretical, Empirical, and Clinical Status of Adaptive and Maladaptive Perfectionism," *Behaviour Change* 30 (2013): 96–116.

2-Blankstein Kirk R. et al., "Dimensions of perfectionism and irrational fears: An examination with the fear survey schedule," *Personality and Individual Differences* 15 (1993): 323–328.

3-Milyavskaya Marina et al., "Fear of missing out: prevalence, dynamics, and consequences of experiencing FOMO," *Motivation and Emotion* 42 (2018): 725–737.

4-Nelson Sara C., "Possum In The Pastries: Viral Image Shows Greedy Marsupial's Bakery Break-In... Or Does It?," *Huffington Post UK* (2012), accessed March 2022.

5-Yin Henry H., Ostlund Sean B., Balleine Bernard W., "Reward-guided learning beyond dopamine in the nucleus accumbens: the integrative functions of cortico-basal ganglia networks," *European Journal of Neuroscience* 28 (2008): 1437–1448.

6-Roetzel Peter G., "Information overload in the information age: a review of the literature from business administration, business psychology, and related disciplines with a bibliometric approach and framework development," *Business Research* 12 (2019): 479–522.

7-Bohn Roger, Short James, "Measuring Consumer Information," *International Journal of Communication* 6 (2012): 980-1000.

8-Miller George A., "The magical number seven, plus or minus two: Some limits on our capacity for processing information," *Psychological Review* 63 (1956): 81-97.

9-Ericsson K. Anders, Chase William G., "Exceptional memory," *American Scientist* 70 (1982): 607-615.

Bibliography

10-Driver, Michael J., Brousseau Kenneth R., Hunsaker Phillip L., *The Dynamic Decision Maker* (1990, 1999)

11-Gross James J., John Oliver P., "Individual differences in two emotion regulation processes: implications for affect, relationships and well-being," *Journal of Personality and Social Psychology* 85 (2003): 348-362.

Chapter 2

1-Ovsiankina Maria, "Untersuchungen zur Handlungs-und Affektpsychologie," *Psychologische Forschung* 11 (1928): 302–379.

2-Syrek Christine J. et al., "Zeigarnik's sleepless nights: How unfinished tasks at the end of the week impair employee sleep on the weekend through rumination," *Journal of Occupational Health Psychology* 22 (2017): 225-238. Weigelt Oliver, Syrek Christine J., "Ovsiankina's Great Relief: How Supplemental Work during the Weekend May Contribute to Recovery in the Face of Unfinished Tasks," *International Journal of Environmental Research and Public Health* 14 (2017): 1606.

3-Clance Pauline R., Imes Suzanne A., "The Impostor Phenomenon in High Achieving Women: Dynamics and Therapeutic Intervention," *Psychotherapy: Theory, Research & Practice* 15 (1978): 241–247.

4-"Michelle Obama: 'I still have impostor syndrome,'" *BBC News UK* (2018), accessed March 2022.

5-Cannon Brookes Mike, "How you can use impostor syndrome to your benefit," *TEDxSydney* (2017), accessed March 2022.

6-Most Steven B., et al., "How not to be seen: the contribution of similarity and selective ignoring to sustained inattentional blindness," *Psychological Science* 12 (2001): 9–17.

7-Benson A.J., et al., "Potential Reductions in Crashes, Injuries, and Deaths from Large-Scale Deployment of Advanced Driver Assistance

Systems (Research Brief)," *AAA Foundation for Traffic Safety* (2018), accessed March 2022.

8-Kruglanski Arie W., *The psychology of closed-mindedness* (Psychology Press, 2004).

9-Wolf Katrin M., Mieg Harald A., "Cognitive determinants of the success of inventors: Complex problem solving and deliberate use of divergent and convergent thinking," *European Journal of Cognitive Psychology* 22 (2010): 443-462.

10-Colzato Lorenza S., Steenbergen Laura, Hommel Bernhard, "Rumination impairs the control of stimulus-induced retrieval of irrelevant information, but not attention, control, or response selection in general," *Psychological Research* 84 (2020): 204–216.

11-Wronska, Marta K., et al., "Person-task fit: Emotional consequences of performing divergent versus convergent thinking tasks depend on need for cognitive closure," *Personality and Individual Differences* 142 (2019): 172-178.

12-Zhong Chen-Bo., Dijksterhuis Ap, Galinsky Adam D., "The merits of unconscious thought in creativity," *Psychological Science* 19 (2008): 912-918.

13-Flaherty Alice W., "Frontotemporal and dopaminergic control of idea generation and creative drive." *The Journal of Comparative Neurology* 493 (2005): 147–153.

14-Oppezzo Marily, Schwartz Daniel L., "Give your ideas some legs: The positive effect of walking on creative thinking." *Journal of Experimental Psychology: Learning, Memory, and Cognition* 40 (2014): 1142-1152.

15-Root-Bernstein Robert, et al., "Arts Foster Scientific Success: Avocations of Nobel, National Academy, Royal Society, and Sigma Xi Members," *Journal of Psychology of Science and Technology* 1 (2008): 51-63.

16-Grossmann Igor, "Wisdom in Context," *Perspectives on Psychological Science* 12 (2017): 233–257.

Chapter 3

1-Brand Paul, Yancey Philip, *Pain: The Gift Nobody Wants* (HarperCollins Publishers, 1993).

2-Cheng Sen, Werning Markus, Suddendorf Thomas, "Dissociating Memory Traces and Scenario Construction in Mental Time Travel," *Neuroscience & Biobehavioral Reviews* 60 (2016): 82–89.

3-Suddendorf Thomas, Bulley A., Miloyan B., "Prospection and natural selection," *Current Opinion in Behavioral Sciences* 24 (2018): 26–31.

4-Roese Neal J., "The Functional Theory of Counterfactual Thinking: New Evidence, New Challenges, New Insights," *Advances in Experimental Social Psychology* 56 (2018): 1–79.

5-Roese Neal J., "The Functional Theory of Counterfactual Thinking: New Evidence, New Challenges, New Insights," *Advances in Experimental Social Psychology* 56 (2018): 1–79. Barnett M. D., Martinez B., "Optimists: it could have been worse; pessimists: it could have been better. Dispositional optimism and pessimism and counterfactual thinking", *Personality and Individual Differences* 86 (2015): 122–125. Walsh N., Egan S.M.,"Things Could Have Been Worse: The Counterfactual Nature Of Gratitude", *26th AIAI Irish Conference on Artificial Intelligence and Cognitive Science* (2018)

6-Hedgcock William M., Luangrath Andrea W., Webster Raelyn, "Counterfactual thinking and facial expressions among Olympic medalists: A conceptual replication of Medvec, Madey, and Gilovich's (1995) findings," *Journal of Experimental Psychology: General* 150 (2021): e13–e21.

7-Roese Neal J., "The Functional Theory of Counterfactual Thinking: New Evidence, New Challenges, New Insights," *Advances in Experimental Social Psychology* 56 (2018): 1–79.

8-West E., Meterko V., "Innocence Project: DNA Exonerations, 1989-2014: Review of data and findings from the first 25 years," The Innocence Project (2016), accessed March 2022.

9-Yurica Carrie L., DiTomasso Robert A., "Cognitive Distortions," *Encyclopedia of Cognitive Behavior Therapy* (2005): 117–122.

10-Gilovich Thomas, Medvec Victoria H., Savitsky Kenneth, "The spotlight effect in social judgment: An egocentric bias in estimates of the salience of one's own actions and appearance," *Journal of Personality and Social Psychology* 78 (2000): 211–222.

11-Roese, Neal J., et al., "Repetitive Regret, Depression, and Anxiety: Findings from a Nationally Representative Survey," *Journal of Social and Clinical Psychology* 28 (2009): 671–688.

12-Stanley Matthew L., et al.,"Emotional intensity in episodic autobiographical memory and counterfactual thinking." *Consciousness and Cognition* 48 (2017): 283–291.

13-Roese, Neal J., Morrison Mike, "Counterfactual Thinking as a Scientific Method," *Historical Social Research* 34 (2009): 16–26.

14-Whitehouse Christiane E., et al., "Comorbid anxiety, depression, and cognition in MS and other immune-mediated disorders," *Neurology* 92 (2019): e406–e417.

15-Ma Xiao., et al., "The Effect of Diaphragmatic Breathing on Attention, Negative Affect and Stress in Healthy Adults," *Frontiers in psychology* 8 (2017).

Chapter 4

1-Parekj Ranna, "What Is Mental Illness," *American Psychiatric Association* (2018), accessed March 2022.

2-Kolubinski Daniel C., Nikčević Ana V. & Spada Marcantonio M., "The Effect of State and Trait Self-Critical Rumination on Acute Distress: An Exploratory Experimental Investigation," *Journal of Rational-Emotive & Cognitive-Behavior Therapy* 39 (2021): 306–321.

3-Festinger Leon, "Cognitive dissonance," *Scientific American* 207 (1962): 93–102.

4-Fotuhi Omid, et al., "Patterns of cognitive dissonance-reducing beliefs among smokers: a longitudinal analysis from the International Tobacco Control (ITC) Four Country Survey," *Tobacco Control* 22 (2013): 52–58.

5-McCoy Sue B., et al., "Perceptions of smoking risk as a function of smoking status," *Journal of Behavioral Medicine* 15 (1992): 469–488.

6-Watkins Edward R., Roberts Henrietta, "Reflecting on rumination: Consequences, causes, mechanisms and treatment of rumination," *Behaviour Research and Therapy* 127 (2020).

7-Nolen-Hoeksema Susan, "The role of rumination in depressive disorders and mixed anxiety/depressive symptoms," *Journal of Abnormal Psychology* 109 (2000): 504–511.

8-Olatunji Bunmi O., Naragon-Gainey Kristin, & Wolitzky-Taylor Kate B., "Specificity of rumination in anxiety and depression: A multimodal meta-analysis," *Clinical Psychology: Science and Practice* 20 (2013): 225–257.

9-Guastella Adam J., Moulds Michelle L., "The impact of rumination on sleep quality following a stressful life event," *Personality and Individual Differences* 42 (2007): 1151–1162.

10-Zoccola Peggy M., Dickerson Sally S., Zaldivar Frank P., "Rumination and cortisol responses to laboratory stressors," *Psychosomatic Medicine* 70 (2008): 661–667.

11-Padgett David, Glaser Ronald, "How stress influences the immune response," *Trends in Immunology* 24 (2003): 444–448.

12-Zoccola Peggy M., et al., "Differential effects of poststressor rumination and distraction on cortisol and C-reactive protein," *Health Psychology* 33 (2014): 1606–1609.

13-Wegner Daniel M., Schneider David J., "The White Bear Story," *Psychological Inquiry* 14 (2003): 326–329.

14-Buck Ross, Powers Stacie R. "The Expression, Communication, and Regulation of Biological Emotions: Sex and Cultural Differences and Similarities," *Psychologia* 48 (2005): 335-353. Fischer Agneta H., Manstead Antony S.R., "The relation between gender and emotion in different cultures", *Gender and emotion: Social psychology perspective* (2000): 71-96.

15-Flynn Jessica J., Hollenstein Tom, Mackey Allisson, "The effect of suppressing and not accepting emotions on depressive symptoms: Is suppression different for men and women?" *Personality and Individual Differences* 49 (2003): 582–586. Hosie Judith A., Milne Alan B., McArthur Lorna, "The after-effects of regulating anger and anger-related emotions on self-report ratings and behavior: Divergent consequences for men and women," *Psychologia* 48 (2005): 288-305.

16-Cutuli Debora, "Cognitive reappraisal and expressive suppression strategies role in the emotion regulation: an overview on their modulatory effects and neural correlates," *Frontiers in Systems Neuroscience* (2014).

17-Gross James J., John Oliver P., "Individual differences in two emotion regulation processes: Implications for affect, relationships, and well-being," *Journal of Personality and Social Psychology* 85 (2003): 348–362.

18-Payer Doris E., et al., "Overlapping neural substrates between intentional and incidental down-regulation of negative emotions," *Emotion* 12 (2012): 229-235.

19-Selye Hans, *Stress Without Distress* (Lippincott Williams & Wilkins, 1974).

20-"Understanding the stress response: Chronic activation of this survival mechanism impairs health," *Harvard Medical School* (2020), accessed March 2022.

21-Kerr Gretchen, Leith Larry, "Stress Management and Athletic Performance," *The Sport Psychologist* 7 (1993): 221–231.

22-Aschbacher Kirstin, et al., "Good stress, bad stress and oxidative stress: Insights from anticipatory cortisol reactivity," *Psychoneuroendocrinology* 38 (2013): 1698–1708.

23-Hanson Sarah, Jones Andy, "Is there evidence that walking groups have health benefits? A systematic review and meta-analysis," *British Journal of Sports Medicine* 49 (2015): 710–715.

Chapter 5

1-Giddens Anthony, *Modernity and Self-Identity: Self and Society in the Late Modern Age* (Stanford University Press, 1991).

2-Markus Hazel, "Self-schemata and information processing about the self," *Journal of Personality and Social Psychology* 35 (1977): 63-78.

3-James McIntosh, Neil McKegane, "Addicts' narratives of recovery from drug use: constructing a non-addict identity," *Social Science & Medicine* 50 (2000): 1501–1510.

4-Freud Sigmund, Strachey James, Freud Anna, *The standard edition of the complete psychological works of Sigmund Freud,* (Hogarth Press, 1957).

5-Baumeister Roy F., "Lying to yourself: The enigma of self-deception". (1993):166-183, in *Lying and deception in everyday life*, Edited by Lewis Michael, Saarni Carolyn

6-Gámez Wakiza, et al., "Development of a measure of experiential avoidance: The Multidimensional Experiential Avoidance Questionnaire," *Psychological Assessment* 23 (2011): 692–713.

7-Camberato Joe, "2019 Small Business Failure Rate: Startup Statistics by Industry," *National Business Capital and Services* (2020), accessed March 2022.

8-Governement français, "Étude d'impact du projet de loi relatif à l'organisation et à la transformation du système de santé," *Légifrance* (2019), accessed March 2022.

Chapter 6

1-Ware Bronnie., *The Top Five Regrets of the Dying: A Life Transformed by the Dearly Departing* (Hay House, 2011).

2-Gilovich Thomas, Medvec Victoria H., "The experience of regret: What, when, and why," *Psychological Review* 102 (1995): 379–395.

3-Savitsky Kenneth, Medvec Victoria H., Gilovich Thomas, "Remembering and regretting: The Zeigarnik effect and the cognitive availability of regrettable actions and inactions," *Personality and Social Psychology Bulletin* 23 (1997): 248–257.

4-Jobs Steve, "Steve Jobs' 2005 Stanford Commencement Address," *Stanford Channel—Youtube* (2005), accessed March 2022.

5-Obukhova L. F., Korepanova I. A., "The Zone of Proximal Development: A Spatiotemporal Model," *Journal of Russian & East European Psychology* 47 (2009): 25–47.

6-Bempechat Janine, London Perry, Dweck Carol S., "Children's conceptions of ability in major domains: An interview and experimental study," *Child Study Journal* 21 (1991): 11–36.

7-Dweck Carol S., *Mindset: The New Psychology of Success* (Random House, 2006).

8-McRaven William H., "University of Texas at Austin 2014 Commencement Address," *Texas Exes—Youtube* (2014), accessed March 2022.

9-Westbrook Andrew, Braver Todd S., "Dopamine does double duty in motivating cognitive effort," *Neuron* 89 (2016): 695–710.

10-Breines Juliana G., Chen Serena, "Self-Compassion Increases Self-Improvement Motivation," *Society for Personality and Social Psychology* 38 (2012): 1133-1143. Neff Kristin, "Self-Compassion: An Alternative Conceptualization of a Healthy Attitude Toward Oneself," *Self and Identity* 2 (2003): 85–101.

11-Neff Kristin D., Germer Christopher, *Oxford Handbook of Compassion Science*, Chap. 27: Self-Compassion and Psychological Wellbeing (Oxford University Press, 2017).

The Third Myth: Overthinking is Inevitable in Decision-Making

1-Duhigg Charles, *The Power of Habit: Why We Do What We Do in Life and Business* (Random House Trade Paperbacks, 2014).

2-Tricomi Elizabeth, Balleine Bernard W., O'Doherty John P., "A specific role for posterior dorsolateral striatum in human habit learning," *European Journal of Neuroscience* 29 (2009): 2225-2232.

Chapter 7

1-Baron Jonathan, Hershey John C., "Outcome bias in decision evaluation," *Journal of Personality and Social Psychology* 54 (1988): 569–579.

2-Kahneman Daniel, *Thinking, Fast and Slow* (Penguin Random House, 2012).

3-Dorey Bruce R., *Lift: The Nature and Craft of Expert Coaching* (Langer Bell Press, 2018).

Chapter 8

1-Wansink Brian, Sobal Jeffery, "Mindless Eating: The 200 Daily Food Decisions We Overlook," *Environment and Behavior* 39 (2007): 106–123.

2-Vohs Kathleen D, et al., "Making choices impairs subsequent self-control: A limited-resource account of decision making, self-regulation, and active initiative," *Journal of Personality and Social Psychology* 94 (2008): 883–898.

3-Samuelson William, Zeckhauser Richard, "Status quo bias in decision making," *Journal of Risk and Uncertainty* 1 (1988): 7–59.

4-O'Hare M H., Bacow L, Sanderson D., "Facility siting and public opposition," United States.

5-Tversky Amos, Kahneman Daniel, "Advances in prospect theory: Cumulative representation of uncertainty," *Journal of Risk and Uncertainty* 5 (1992): 297–323.

6-Parayre Roch, "The strategic implications of sunk costs: A behavioral perspective," *Journal of Economic Behavior and Organization* 28 (1995): 417–442.

7-Ferris Tim, "General Stan McChrystal on Eating One Meal Per Day, Special Ops, and Mental Toughness," *The Tim Ferris* Show #86 (2015).

8-Hastorf Albert H., Cantrill Hadley, "They saw a game; a case study," *Journal of Abnormal Psychology* 49 (1995): 129–134.

9-Gilbert Daniel T.; Ebert Jane E.J., "Decisions and revisions: The affective forecasting of changeable outcomes," *Journal of Personality and Social Psychology* 82 (2002): 503–514.

10-"Cortés Burns His Boats," PBS.org, accessed March 2022.

Chapter 9

1-Chang Ruth, "How To Make Hard Choices" *TED* (2014), accessed March 2022.

2-Rosen Frederick, *Classical Utilitarianism from Hume to Mill* (Routledge, 2003).

3-Kant Immanuel., *Groundwork of the Metaphysic of Morals*, translated by Ellington James W. (Hackett, 1993).

4-Awad Edmond; et al., "Universals and variations in moral decisions made in 42 countries by 70,000 participants," *PNAS* 117 (2020).

5-Gold Natalie, Colman Andrew M., Pulford Briony D., "Cultural differences in responses to real-life and hypothetical trolley problems," *Judgment and Decision Making* 9 (2014): 65–76.

6-Brown Dwayne, Buis Alan, "NASA Selects Student's Entry as New Mars Rover Name," *NASA* (2009), accessed March 2022.

7-Villanueva G. L., et al., "Strong water isotopic anomalies in the martian atmosphere: Probing current and ancient reservoirs," *Science* 348 (2014): 218–221.

8-Eurich Tasha, *Insight: The Power of Self-Awareness in a Self-Deluded World* (Pan Macmillan, 2017).

Conclusion of the Third Myth

1-Epstein Seymour, "Demystifying intuition: What it is, what it does, and how it does it," *Psychological Inquiry* 21 (2010): 295–312.

2-Kahneman Daniel, "The Psychology of Intuitive Judgment and Choices", Annual World Business Forum NYC (2018).

3-Gigerenzer Gerd, "How do smart people make smart decisions?" *TEDxTalks—Youtube* (2017), accessed March 2022.

Conclusion

1-Baguley David, McFerran Don, Hall Deborah, "Tinnitus," *The Lancet* 382 (2013): 1600–1607. Andersson Gerhard, "Psychological aspects of tinnitus and the application of cognitive-behavioral therapy," *Clinical Psychology Review* 22 (2002): 977–990.

www.ingramcontent.com/pod-product-compliance
Lightning Source LLC
Chambersburg PA
CBHW022055290426
44109CB00014B/1101